THE LIE OF THE LAND

Aspects of the Archaeology and
History of the Designed Landscape
in the South West of England

The Lie of the Land

Aspects of the Archaeology and
History of the Designed Landscape
in the South West of England

Edited by

Robert Wilson-North

THE MINT PRESS

Devon
Gardens
Trust

First published in Great Britain by
The Mint Press and the Devon Gardens Trust, 2003

© Robert Wilson-North and the several contributors,
each in respect of the material contributed, 2003

ISBN 1-903356-22-9

Cataloguing in Publication Data
CIP record for this title is available from the British
Library

The Mint Press
18 The Mint
Exeter, Devon
England EX4 3BL

Designed and typeset in Sabon 9.5/11.5 by
Mike Dobson, Quince Typesetting

Cover design by Delphine Jones

Printed and bound in Great Britain
by Short Run Press Ltd, Exeter

Contents

Acknowledgements

The Lie of the Land has its origins in a conference held in Exeter in 1998 under the auspices of the Centre for South Western Historical Studies. The conference, whose primary purpose was to illustrate the potential of garden archaeology in South West England, was the idea of Todd Gray, but was realised through the organisational skills and energy of Michelle Marr (formerly Gregory). New discoveries, innovative approaches to designed landscapes and the integration of historical and archaeological methods characterised the conference, and led to the decision to bring together permanently such a seminal body of material.

The production of the book would not have been possible without the commitment and co-operation of all the contributors. Its publication has been generously supported by the Devon Gardens Trust and the National Lottery Awards for All. I am especially grateful to Todd Gray for his assistance with editorial matters, to Mike Dobson for the design and typesetting and to Delphine Jones who designed the front cover.

The Lie of the Land seeks to advance the study of designed landscapes in south west England; the breadth of its content and the examples cited in these pages should inspire all those with an interest in garden history and the history of the landscape to seek out such places. Investigating the remains of designed landscapes helps us to gain an insight into the minds and aspirations of those who changed, manipulated – for pleasure – the distinctive and beautiful landscape of the West Country.

> Everything passes and vanishes;
> Everything leaves its trace;
> And often you see in a footstep
> What you could not see in a face.
>
> (*William Allingham, 1882*)

Contributors

James Bond worked as a field archaeologist in the county museum services of Worcestershire and Oxfordshire before turning freelance and moving to North Somerset in 1986. He is currently a Visiting Fellow in the Archaeology Department at the University of Bristol. His publications include studies of the landscape of Blenheim Park and the parks and gardens of Somerset.

James Bond
The Anchorage
Coast Road
Walton-in-Gordano
Clevedon
North Somerset BS21 7AR
jimserf@aol.com

Christopher Currie is an archaeological consultant. He has a particular interest in garden archaeology and has directed the excavations at Dartington Hall.

Christopher Currie
CKC Archaeology
71 Upper Barn Close
Fair Oak
Hampshire SO50 8DB
CCurrie260@aol.com

Brian Dix specializes in archaeology for the conservation of historic gardens and designed landscapes. His projects in the UK include the reconstruction of William III's Privy Garden at Hampton Court Palace, and he has worked in Transylvania and Russia as well as at other European sites. He lectures widely and teaches part-time at the Architectural Association Graduate School.

Brian Dix
37 Lime Avenue
Northampton NN3 2HA
briandix@privygarden.freeserve.co.uk

Paul Everson is Head of Archaeological Investigation with English Heritage, having worked for the Royal Commission on the Historical Monuments of England before the merger of the two state agencies. He has surveyed the field evidence of a number of abandoned (and living) gardens of dates ranging from the twelfth century to Gertrude Jekyll's own garden at Munstead Wood. More especially he has taken a leading interest in the nature of gardens and designed landscapes of the medieval period, and in the symbolism of gardens and their relationship to the buildings they accompanied. He has published both accounts of individual sites and wider discussions on these themes.

Paul Everson
English Heritage
National Monuments Record Centre
Great Western Village
Kemble Drive
Swindon SN2 2GZ
paul.everson@english-heritage.org.uk

June Fenwick is a Garden Recorder for the Cornwall Gardens Trust. Having always a deep interest in garden history, she has been a member of the Cornwall Gardens Trust since 1989. She previously trained and worked in garden design in the 1980s. She is a past Chairman of Recorders and is currently researching for the Cornwall Gardens Trust and working on garden cataloguing.

> June Fenwick
> Treetops
> Helford
> Helston
> Cornwall TR12 6JZ
> Junedfenwick@aol.com

Peter Herring is a Principal Archaeologist in the Historic Environment Service of Cornwall County Council, and has been recording and interpreting Cornwall's historic landscape since the late 1970s. He has a particular interest in helping communities value their local historic environment, being closely involved with the pilot historic landscape characterization undertaken in Cornwall in 1994.

> Peter Herring
> Historic Environment Service
> Cornwall County Council
> Kennal Building
> Old County Hall
> Station Road
> TRURO
> Cornwall TR1 3EX
> pherring@cornwall.gov.uk

Dr Ian Hewitt is Archaeological Research Projects Manager at Bournemouth University and lectures in medieval and post-medieval archaeology. He has recently completed a five-year survey of the archaeological potential of rural settlements in Hampshire on behalf of Hampshire County Council.

> Ian Hewitt
> Bournemouth University
> School of Conservation Sciences
> Fern Barrow,
> POOLE BH12 5BB
> ihewitt@bournemouth.ac.uk

Jonathan Lovie is an historic landscape consultant who has been employed since 1998 as one of the Inspectors of Historic Parks and Gardens at English Heritage. He has particular responsibility for the revision of the *Register of Parks and Gardens of Special Historic Interest* in the south-west of England and in parts of the Midlands, and has published studies of several historic designed landscapes in these areas.

> Jonathan Lovie
> 88 Dunchurch Road
> Rugby
> Warwickshire CV22 6AE

Dr Alison A. Newton is a retired University Lecturer in Biochemistry at Cambridge University, and Fellow Emerita of Newnham College, Cambridge. She is a Garden Recorder for both the Devon and Cornwall Gardens Trusts.

> Dr Alison A. Newton
> Rosemarsland
> Gooseham
> Bude
> Cornwall EX23 9PQ

Martin Papworth is the archaeologist for the National Trust's Wessex Region. Previously he worked for Wessex Archaeology. His involvement with abandoned gardens began with a survey of Maori cultivation terraces in Northland, New Zealand.

> Martin Papworth
> The National Trust
> Wessex Regional Office
> Eastleigh Court
> Bishopstrow
> Warminster
> Wiltshire BA12 9HW
> whbmdp@smtp.ntrust.org.uk

Hazel Riley is a field archaeologist and works as a Field Investigator at the Exeter Office of English Heritage. Previously she worked for the Royal Commission on the Historical Monuments of England, and has surveyed sites of all periods across south-west England.

Hazel Riley
English Heritage
5 Marlborough Court
Manaton Close
Marsh Barton
Exeter EX2 8PF

Robert Waterhouse (BA) is a freelance archaeologist, specializing in buildings, as well as industrial and landscape archaeology. He has worked for the National Trust Vernacular Buildings Survey and English Heritage's Monument Protection Programme. He now advises South Hams and Teignbridge District Councils on archaeological matters. He is currently carrying out further research, survey and excavation on the important garden at Shilston Barton, Modbury. In addition to his interest in historic gardens, he is currently engaged in research on Devon's medieval and post-medieval mansion houses and their environs, for a forthcoming book.

Robert Waterhouse
13 Mill Meadow
Ashburton
Devon TQ13 7RN

Eileen Wilkes (Ms) is undertaking PhD research at Bournemouth University. Her specialist interest is late prehistoric sites on the English Channel coast.

Eileen Wilkes
Bournemouth University
School of Conservation Sciences
Fern Barrow,
POOLE BH12 5BB
ewilkes@bournemouth.ac.uk

Rob Wilson-North is the archaeologist for the Exmoor National Park Authority. Previously he worked for the Royal Commission on the Historical Monuments of England for 15 years. He has surveyed abandoned gardens in a number of counties across England, most recently in the south-west. He has published the relict gardens at Stowe (Cornwall), as well as Low Ham and Witham (both in Somerset).

Rob Wilson-North
Exmoor National Park Authority
Exmoor House
Dulverton
Somerset TA22 9HL
rwilson-north@exmoor-nationalpark.gov.uk

Approaches to Garden Archaeology and Designed Landscapes in South West England

Robert Wilson-North

The National Scene

Before the 1980s historic parks and gardens had largely been the domain of garden historians and to a lesser extent, landscape architects. When archaeologists strayed into these polite landscapes it was usually because they had another reason to be there. An eighteenth-century park might contain the humps and bumps of a deserted medieval village; the earthworks of a lost seventeenth-century water parterre were only examined because they had been misidentified as the remains of a medieval moated manor. Indeed it was precisely because of instances like this that archaeologists began to look at the remains of designed landscapes in their own right. Since those early days, garden archaeology has matured from a fledgling discipline. It has become a respected tool in the armoury of anyone concerned with the investigation, interpretation and conservation of historic gardens. Landmarks in the establishment of the discipline have been the few seminal national publications which have set out garden archaeology's stall, such as Chris Taylor's *The Archaeology of*

Gardens (1983) in the Shire Archaeology series and the Council for British Archaeology's *Garden Archaeology* (Brown 1991). The publication of the Strawberry Hill conference (Jacques 1995) embodied a wider recognition of the contribution of garden archaeology. *There By Design* (Pattison 1998) highlighted the fruitful and welcome collaboration of distinct organisations, which brought together traditional, archaeological field survey and garden history with the Royal Commission on the Historical Monuments of England and the Garden History Society. Publication of individual projects has also contributed to a greater awareness of the subject, and is a credit to the energy of some fieldworkers (Williamson 1995 and 1996 for examples). In some areas, publications have appeared which draw together recent work across one county, for example. The last 20 years have indeed been a fruitful time. It has seen a sharing of different approaches and methodologies, which has enabled the rich seam of designed landscapes – such a ubiquitous feature of the English landscape – to be mined more effectively.

In the South West, a regional focus was

achieved through a conference organised in Exeter in 1998 by the Devon Gardens Trust and the Centre for South-Western Historical Studies. This brought together the work of individuals and organisations working on historic gardens, and sought to emphasise the place of garden archaeology in the study of historic gardens in the South West.

The Nature of the Evidence

Two designed landscapes reflect both the variety of the evidence and the challenge it presents. They underpin the value of an interdisciplinary approach.

Castle Hill near South Molton is a fine seventeenth-century house within a landscape park complete with former lake and canal, a remarkable range of parkland buildings, temples, bridges and a fine triumphal arch (Fig. 1). The park and house have evolved over several centuries, culminating in the richness we see today. It has been studied by garden historians and landscape consultants and a management plan was completed, providing the basis for an ambitious restoration project.

Castle Hill contrasts well with Stowe in north Cornwall (Fig. 2). Here the house was short-lived and nothing now survives. It was built by the Grenville family in 1689 and was surrounded by elaborate formal gardens within a rigid series of walled compartments. The house and garden were disused by 1701, and everything demolished by 1740. The house and gardens, however, can be revealed through a combination of good contemporary map sources and pictorial evidence. These are complemented by the complete preservation of the field archaeology: garden terraces, flower beds and paths all survive as earthworks. This combination of sources of evidence which can be tested against each other and applied to a house of such short duration, provide a rare insight into a lavish Restoration house and garden (Wilson-North 1993).

Castle Hill, then, is the archetypal elegant English parkland, displaying a vibrant continuity of use to the present day; in contrast, Stowe is caught in time – a snapshot of a late seventeenth-century high status house and its setting.

Fig. 1 Castle Hill, South Molton Devon. The Triumphal Arch.
(© Robert Wilson-North)

Fig. 2 Stowe, Cornwall. The earthworks of the seventeenth century home and gardens of the Grenville family (© Robert Wilson-North)

Such is the variety of the evidence before us, and yet it is possible to look at a landscape such as Castle Hill through a methodology that values equally the evidence on the ground (the archaeology) and the historical.

The South West of England – Background

The South West of England has a diverse and beautiful natural landscape, combined with a favourable climate. In these conditions, people have created gardens in practically every part of the peninsula.

Here, as elsewhere in England, historic gardens and designed landscapes have traditionally been looked at through the eyes of the historian only. This is no longer the case. The seed change is partly reflected in the published county gardens surveys; the earliest of these reflect the lack of archaeological fieldwork, whilst the more recent examples show a more integrated approach to the subject. Devon was the first: *Devon Gardens, an Historical Survey* (Pugsley 1994), Cornwall and Somerset fol-

lowed suit with comprehensive surveys (Pett 1998 and Bond 1998 respectively).

Research and fieldwork on individual gardens and designed landscapes has been fruitful. Examples are Cynthia Gaskell-Brown's work at Mount Edgcumbe in Cornwall, Philip White's work at Hestercombe in Somerset and Christopher Currie's excavations at Dartington Hall in Devon (this volume). James Bond's fieldwork in Somerset (this volume) formed the basis for the county survey. Research by consultancy organisations for restoration projects like Castle Hill, South Molton, has also played an important role. The County Garden Trusts are very active gathering information on individual gardens. Lastly fieldwork undertaken by the former Royal Commission on the Historical Monuments of England (now merged with English Heritage) has clearly demonstrated the key role that traditional earthwork survey can play in recovering the plan and detailed arrangements of lost gardens (e.g. Wilson-North 1998). The incidence of archaeological fieldwork in South West England is characterised by its haphazardness. It reflects two overarching factors. Firstly the enthusiastic commitment of individual fieldworkers, wherever they happen to be working, and secondly, the incidence of individual restoration projects.

The Scope of this Book

The purpose of this book is to introduce the contribution that archaeology can make to the study of designed landscapes in their broadest sense. It presents a slice – both topographically and methodologically – across garden archaeology in South West England. In its scope, it deals with everything from small-scale excavation to synthetic surveys of whole counties. It presents a number of gardens and designed landscapes that are known only from the archaeological evidence and would not otherwise be known to the garden historian. The source material of garden archaeology in the West Country is very diverse and that variety is reflected in the pages of this book.

For those not familiar with garden archaeology, this piece gives an overview of the subject and work in the South West. Jonathan Lovie then describes the work of the Parks and Gardens Register, the principal tool for the protection of nationally important parks and gardens. Martin Papworth reviews recent excavations on National Trust historic gardens such as Kingston Lacey, Barrington Court, Lacock Abbey and Montacute. Brian Dix's piece sets the national context. Paul Everson describes the national evidence for medieval designed landscapes with a series of stunning examples, and he shows the potential that the South West has to add to this collection.

Peter Herring describes the evidence for medieval deer parks in Cornwall and gives a vivid account both of their impact on the medieval landscape and the ways they were used to impress and overawe. Christopher Currie describes the recent excavations at Dartington Hall, and for the first time the extraordinary 'theatre of water' at Shilston Barton is published. Robert Waterhouse describes the newly discovered evidence for sixteenth and seventeenth-century gardens in south Devon against the compelling and often tantalising architectural remains. James Bond adds to his county survey of Somerset. Hazel Riley and I set out

the evidence for an abandoned seventeenth-century house and water garden overlooked by the famous Cerne Abbas giant in Dorset. Ian Hewitt and Eileen Wilkes explore aspects of a designed landscape in Dorset, and in so doing, uncover surprising evidence for the cuckoo in Dorset place-names.

The work of the county Garden Trusts is represented by two sites recorded by the Cornwall Gardens Trust: June Fenwick describes the remarkable twentieth-century garden at The Downes, overlooking the Hayle estuary, and Alison A. Newton sets out the evidence for the unusual nineteenth-century walled garden at Morval.

References

Bond, J. 1998 *Somerset Parks and Gardens*

Brown, T. 1991 *Garden Archaeology* CBA Research Report No. 78

Jacques, D. 1997 (ed.) *The Techniques and Uses of Garden Archaeology* in *Journal of Garden History* vol. 17, no. 1, Jan–Mar 1997

Pattison, P. 1998 (ed.) *There By Design Field Archaeology in Parks and Gardens*

Pett, D.E. 1998 *The Parks and Gardens of Cornwall*

Pugsley, S. 1994 *Devon Gardens An Historical Survey*

Taylor, C.C. 1983 *The Archaeology of Gardens*

Williamson, T. 1995 *Polite Landscapes: Gardens and Society in 18th century England*

Williamson, T. 1996 'Roger North at Rougham: a lost house and its landscape' in C. Rawcliffe, R. Virgoe and R. Wilson (eds) *Counties and Communities: Essays on East Anglian History presented to Hassell Smith*, 275–90

Wilson-North, W.R. 1993 'Stowe: the country house and garden of the Grenville family' *Cornish Archaeol.* 32, 112–127

Wilson-North, W.R. 1998 'Two relict gardens in Somerset: their changing fortunes through the 17th and 18th centuries as revealed by the field evidence and other sources' in P. Pattison (ed.) *There By Design Field Archaeology in Parks and Gardens*, 56–64 (RCHME, British Archaeological Reports, British Series 267)

Identifying Historic Designed Landscapes: The English Heritage Register of Parks and Gardens

Jonathan Lovie

Introduction

It is today widely appreciated that buildings of architectural and historic significance are listed by the Department of Culture, Media and Sport, and that ancient monuments are similarly recorded and protected. It is perhaps less well known that since the 1980s there has been a national record of the historic parks and gardens which contribute to our varied landscape heritage.

The main purpose of the *Register of Parks and Gardens* is to help to ensure that the character which makes these landscapes of national importance can be safeguarded during ongoing management or if any change is planned which could affect them. It is hoped that by drawing attention to sites in this way, English Heritage will increase awareness of their value and encourage those who own them or care for them, to treat these special places with due care.

Today, there are some 1500 sites considered to be of national significance included on the *Register*. These sites are graded in order to give additional guidance as to their significance. The majority of sites identified as being of a sufficiently high standard to merit a national designation are included on the *Register* at grade II. Approximately thirty per cent of the sites on the *Register* are considered to be of exceptional historic interest and are accordingly graded at II*. A further ten per cent of sites are recognised as being of international importance, and are registered at grade I. In the South West this group includes such varied sites as Hestercombe in Somerset with its eighteenth-century landscape and formal gardens by Sir Edwin Lutyens and Gertrude Jekyll; Mount Edgcumbe, Cornwall with its extensive coastal picturesque landscape, and Humphry Repton's great commissions at Endsleigh in Devon and Port Eliot in Cornwall.

Sites of many different types are included in the *Register*, from landscape parks, to town squares and examples of urban planning such as Blaise Hamlet, Bristol (grade II*); public parks such as Royal Victoria Park, Bath (grade II) or Wellington Park, Somerset (grade II); and cemeteries including Arnos Vale Cemetery, Bristol (grade II*), Bath Abbey Cemetery (grade II), and Wimbourne Road Cemetery, Bournemouth (grade II*). Similarly, the age of registered sites varies from Fishbourne Roman Palace, West Sussex (grade II*), to Civic Square, Plymouth (grade II) laid out by Sir Geoffrey Jellicoe in the early 1960s. To be considered for inclusion on the *Register* a site must be more than thirty years old; and the more recent the date of a garden's construction, the more intact it should survive.

More details of the background to the *Register*, and the criteria used to assess sites for inclusion on it are to be found in a booklet, *The Register of Parks and Gardens An Introduction*, published by English Heritage in 1998, available free of charge from Customer Services, NMRC, Kemble Drive, Swindon, SN2 2GZ.

The Register in Practice – The Protection of Historic Parks and Gardens

The inclusion of a site on the *Register* in itself brings no additional statutory controls. However, local authorities are required by central government to make provision for the protection of the historic environment in their policies and allocation of resources. Registration is a material planning consideration in planning terms, so in accordance with government advice contained in Planning Policy Guidance Note 15, paragraph 2.24, local planning and highway authorities must, when determining a planning application which would affect a registered site or its setting, take into account the historic interest of the site. Local plans at district level, and county structure plan policies will also often refer to the protection of registered sites, and such policies have a key role in the planning process.

In addition to guidance in PPG 15, Central Government Circular 9/95 (summarised in Environment Circular 14/97 and Culture, Media and Sport Circular 1/97) requires planning authorities to consult English Heritage where an application affects a grade I or grade II* registered site, and the Garden History Society on

applications affecting registered sites of all grades. It must be emphasised that the duty of consultation contained in Circular 9/95 is a requirement, and not an option; similarly it must always be borne in mind that all sites included on the *Register*, irrespective of grade, have been identified as being of significance to the national cultural heritage. Professional guidance on planning and other issues is provided for English Heritage by the organisation's Regional Landscape Architects; in the South West Region this Officer is based in the Bristol office.

PPG 15 guides planning authorities to make provision for the protection of registered parks and gardens in their development plans (PPG15, paragraphs 1.6 and 2.1). Many local plans now include policies designed to safeguard historic parks and gardens within the area covered. These usually stress in particular registered sites, but the best policies also include 'local lists' which cover designed landscapes which are of local and regional, rather than national significance. The Conservation Officer of the Garden History Society, and the Association of Gardens Trusts will advise local authorities, amenity groups and interested individuals on this important aspect of the local planning process.

Finally, it is important to recognise that the designation of a site on the *Register* may overlap with other statutory and non-statutory designations. A registered site will often contain one or more listed buildings – either the principal building to which the designed landscape relates, or perhaps landscape structures such as temples, summerhouses, terraces, or kitchen garden walls. Sometimes a designed landscape will incorporate a Scheduled Ancient Monument such as Dolbury Camp at Killerton, Devon (grade II*) which was planted with beech trees as a landscape feature by John Veitch in the late eighteenth century. Perhaps one of the most striking examples of the appropriation of an ancient monument as a landscape feature is Sir William Molesworth's use of earthworks as a picturesque feature on his mid nineteenth-century drive at Pencarrow, Cornwall (grade II*). At the same time, a registered garden might lie within, and make a significant contribution to the character of a conservation area designated by the local authority (English Heritage, October 1995, paragraph 3.4). It may also be within an Area of Outstanding Natural Beauty, or have a variety of ecological designations. In relation to the implemented protection of registered sites, it is clear that owners, a variety of amenity and interest groups and statutory bodies should work together and maintain regular dialogue.

The Register and Garden Archaeology

Eastbury, Dorset

Compared to an area such as the East Midlands with its wealth of registered sites whose principal interest lies in their archaeology such as Harrington (grade II*), Holdenby House (grade II*) or Lyveden New Bield (grade II*), the South West appears to have relatively few principally archaeological sites on the *Register*. One particular example, Eastbury in Dorset (grade II*), stands out.

At Eastbury, the archaeological remains are those of an early eighteenth-century formal garden and park landscape which was created for the eccentric and very wealthy George Bubb Doddington by Charles Bridgeman. George Bubb Doddington inherited the estate and an unfinished house by Vanbrugh in 1720 from his uncle (Taylor 1998, 210). Work on the house and gardens proceeded from 1722 until their completion *c.*1738, by which time Eastbury had become a noted literary and artistic centre (Willis 1977, 47). Despite James Thomson's description of Doddington's 'green delightful walks' at Eastbury, 'Where simple nature reigns' (Thomson 1730, ll. 654–6), the plan of Bridgeman's gardens published by Colen Campbell

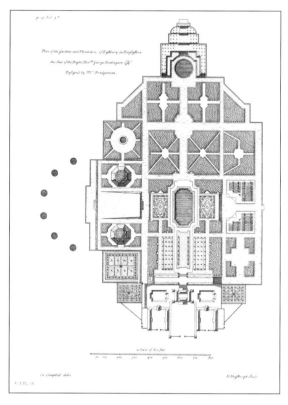

Fig. 3 Eastbury Dorset. Plan of house and gardens in the eighteenth century (from Vitruvius Britannicus)

Fig. 4 Eastbury, Dorset. 'The Great Arch and its fantastic overgrowth' (from RCHME Dorset IV)
(© Crown copyright. NMR)

in *Vitruvius Britannicus* shows a highly formal scheme with an axial vista stretching away from the house across a lawn and along a rectangular canal. The canal was flanked by elaborate parterres, and a north-south cross axis was flanked to the north by a pair of octagonal mounts. The axis of the vista was projected through a wilderness comprising rectangular compartments to a rectangular amphitheatre which rose behind a circular basin which lay in a shallow valley; the amphitheatre was surmounted by a Corinthian temple to designs by Vanbrugh (Taylor 1998, 210). Beyond the gardens, the park was laid out with groves broken into rectangular and triangular areas. To the north of the house the octagonal garden mounts were echoed by fourteen small, tree-covered hillocks which were arranged in two parallel lines stretching across the park (RCHME 1972, 93). Willis notes that Bridgeman's own plans for Eastbury

(Bodleian Library, Gough Maps) are drawn in a freer style than the one published by Campbell, and that the wider park landscape was integrated with the formal garden by the use of ha-has (Willis 1977, 48); similarly, the monumental approach from the west was partly enclosed by a wooded amphitheatre (Willis 1977, 48).

Bubb Doddington, created Lord Melcombe in 1761, died a bachelor in 1762. The estate passed to his relative, Earl Temple of Stowe, Buckinghamshire, who from 1775 demolished the house, leaving only the stables, which were subsequently converted into a residence (*Country Life* 1948). The gardens were finally abandoned in 1782, and the park underwent alteration in the nineteenth century. The Tithe map of 1840 indicates that the western half of the central garden had already been abandoned and converted to arable farmland. The eastern half of the garden survived in an abandoned but intact state until it too was ploughed in 1958 (RCHME 1972, 93). Today some features survive as scarps and earthworks, including the octagonal mounds flanking the north-south vista, the south ha-ha, and some of the hillocks in the park to the north of the garden. Other features show up as crop and soil marks on aerial photographs.

While Eastbury is at present the only registered site in the South West which survives in an almost purely archaeological state, on-going research informed by the experience of archaeologists working on garden sites elsewhere in the country is likely to lead to the identification of further sites of both regional and national significance.

Multi-phased Ornamental Landscapes

The great majority of designed landscapes have evolved over a considerable period of time, and naturally include archaeological remains of features no longer extant above ground. These range from the grassed-over mid nineteenth-century parterre such as that at Pencarrow, Cornwall to the complex series of features at Godolphin, Cornwall (grade II*) which have been the subject of detailed examination by the Cornwall Archaeological Unit (CAU 1997). Here, the great house created by the Godolphin family from the early medieval period was neglected in the early eighteenth century while the family was engaged in London political life. It was almost relegated to the status of a farm house when the estate was inherited by the Duke of Leeds in 1785. The modern landscape around the house retains, frozen within it, a deer park with pillow mounds and other archaeological features on the hill south of the house, terraces and former garden enclosures near the house, and an orchard with what appears to be the remains of a formal layout with raised walks (CAU 1997).

The Cornwall Archaeological Unit's work at Godolphin, and similar studies elsewhere, such as that now being undertaken at Cotehele, Cornwall, underline the importance of archaeology for our understanding and interpretation of historic parks and gardens. Archaeology similarly plays a significant role in the restoration of historic parks and gardens. At Hestercombe, Somerset (grade I) the revelation of the eighteenth-century landscape garden in the combe north of the house has added considerably to

Fig. 5 Hestercombe, Somerset. The Witch House (© Jonathan Lovie)

the significance of what was already a grade I registered site. Archaeology has been vital in allowing lost features such as the Witch House (Fig. 5), the Gothic Seat and several urns to be located and reconstructed in the correct position, thus recreating the series of picturesque incidents and views which are essential to Coplestone Warre Bampfylde's landscape garden (pers. comm. Philip White). A similar process is underway at Endsleigh, Devon (grade I), which demonstrates that at its simplest level, field archaeology can be helpful in locating lost walks, seats and other basic features, the correct understanding of which can be vital to the success of a restoration project.

Elsewhere, archaeology can reveal more about the historic development of a site, perhaps indicating a continuity which is belied by appearances, as at Mount Edgcumbe, Cornwall (grade I). The English Garden House, a rectangular garden building in the pleasure grounds south-east of the house, appears in its present form to date from the late eighteenth or early nineteenth century. However, archaeological investigation by Cynthia Gaskell-Brown and R.W. Humphries has shown that the present building incorporates a much earlier garden structure, which is visible on an early eighteenth century engraving by Thomas Badeslade (Gaskell Brown and Humphries 1993). This engraving also shows that the valley to the south, today the site of Milton's Temple, has evolved from a formal garden known as the amphitheatre. The formal ponds shown by Badeslade to the north-east of the house have also been the subject of archaeological investigation (pers. comm. C. Gaskell-Brown).

In some instances, archaeology can be helpful in dispelling myths which arise, or which are perhaps deliberately propagated, about particular sites. A fascinating example of this phenomenon would be Dartington Hall, Devon (grade II*), where a series of investigations undertaken by Christopher Currie has shown that the feature identified by Dorothy Elmhirst as John Holand's fourteenth-century tiltyard is an early twentieth-century romanticism. The Tiltyard is a wedge-shaped valley broadening to the east, lying to the south of the Hall. It is enclosed to the north by two ramped grass terraces, while to the south there are five similar ramped terraces, above which stands a row of seven sweet chestnuts which have been estimated to be between 300 and 400 years old (Currie 1993). The floor of the valley is level, with steps ascending west to the woodland garden; further steps descend east to the Valley Field. The Tiltyard assumed its present form as late as 1954–55 under the guidance of Percy Cane, when a 1930s open-air theatre at the east end of the valley was levelled (Snell 1989, 62–6, 84). The Elmhirsts believed that the work of 1954–55 restored the Tiltyard to its original form, but late twentieth-century archaeological investigation has proved that the surrounding terraces date from the late sixteenth or seventeenth century, and that the valley floor was not originally at its present level (Currie 1993). This re-evaluation of the Tiltyard makes it no less interesting or significant in a complex site which includes diverse features such as an early fourteenth-century walled deer park and garden features designed by Harry Avray Tipping, Beatrix Farrand and Percy Cane (Snell 1989, 22, 34, 50).

The Way Ahead for the Register

The understanding of garden history and garden archaeology have both advanced considerably over the past twenty years. Accordingly, the *Register* should not be seen as a static document. At present, English Heritage is undertaking two complementary programmes in order to ensure that the information contained in the Register is of the highest quality, and that the sites included accurately reflect our national heritage of historic designed landscapes.

The Register Upgrade Programme aims to produce an updated *Register* by the end of the year 2002. Additional research coupled with site visits, where possible involving the main owners or their agents, will help to confirm the interest and importance of each site. New descriptions are being written which better reflect the historic interest of the site and the reason for its inclusion on the *Register*. The new descriptions should not, however, be seen as a definitive account of the historic development of a particular site. Registered site boundaries and grades will also be checked, producing, it is hoped, an enhanced tool for planners and others involved in the field.

The Register Review Programme has been undertaken in two phases, with initial work in partnership with local authorities and other locally-based organisations concentrating on the compilation of county-based lists of sites which may merit further consideration for inclusion on the *Register*. A second phase, resources permitting programmed for 2001 onwards, will see the detailed assessment of the short-listed sites and, as appropriate, the addition of selected sites to the *Register*.

At the same time, there remains the opportunity for spot-registration, where a site is under imminent threat from proposals which would be prejudicial to its historic interest, or where confirmation of a site's national significance is required in the context of applications for grant funding for restoration or repair. For further information on this process owners, professionals or other interested groups or individuals should contact the Designed Landscapes Team at Room 240, 23 Savile Row, London, W1X 1AB.

While some designed landscapes have become frozen at a particular point of their development, the vast majority of sites have a complex evolution over an extended period. A variety of disciplines, including, crucially, archaeology, is required properly to understand and interpret such sites. This more holistic approach to the historic environment has been recognised by English Heritage in its recent re-organisation, which has placed the *Register of Parks and Gardens* as a national programme alongside the listing of buildings of architectural and historic significance, and the scheduling of ancient monuments. The specialist expertise of colleagues is greatly valued, and it is recognised that in identifying and describing parks and gardens of national significance, archaeological data will be of increasing importance. Suggestions of new sites which can be added to the county lists of sites for future assessment are welcomed together with the professional advice and guidance of archaeologists working in constructive dialogue.

Note

The Register of Parks and Gardens of Special Historic Interest in England was drawn up by English Heritage under powers conferred by Section 8C of the Historic Buildings and Ancient Monuments Act 1953 (inserted by section 33 of, and paragraph 10 of Section 4 to, the National Heritage Act 1983–84) in order to recognise those sites which are of national historic importance.

References

Binney, M. 1984 *Our Vanishing Heritage*

Binney, M. and Hills, A. 1979 *Elysian Gardens*

Bridgeman, C. garden plans for Eastbury, Dorset, early C18, Bodleian Library, Gough Maps vi ff. 93, 94

Campbell, C. 1725 *Vitruvius Britannicus* iii

Country Life 104 (1948), pp. 1386–89

Currie, C.K. 1993 'Excavations in the Gardens of Dartington Hall' unpub. interim report

Department of the Environment and Department of National Heritage September 1994, *Planning Policy Guidance: Planning and the Historic Environment* (PPG15)

English Heritage, October 1995, *Conservation Area Practice*

English Heritage, November 1998, *The Register of Parks and Gardens An Introduction*

Gaskell Brown, C. and Humphries, R.W. 1993 *The English Garden House Mount Edgcumbe: Excavation and Survey*

Herring, P. 1997 'Godolphin Archaeological and Historical Assessment' Cornwall Archaeological Unit

Royal Commission on Historical Monuments (England) *Dorset* IV 1972, 90–93

Snell, R. 1989 *From the Bare Stem Making Dorothy Elmhirst's Garden at Dartington Hall*

Taylor, C.C. 1983 *Archaeology of Gardens*

Taylor, C.C. 1998 *Parks and Gardens of Britain A Landscape History from the Air*

Thomson, J. 1730 *Seasons* – Autumn

Willis, P. 1977 *Charles Bridgeman*

Archaeological Recording on Historic Gardens by The National Trust

Martin Papworth

Introduction

The parks and gardens surrounding the mansion houses owned by the National Trust are managed with the knowledge that they are archaeological landscapes. The Trust's garden advisors seek to present these landscapes in an appropriate form with the realisation that on each site there may have been a number of different garden designs at different periods. With each rebuilding of the mansion, a fashionable garden layout was usually created around it. A new garden design could remove the details of an earlier garden completely or it might retain elements of the earlier layout. Using the evidence from fieldwork and documentary research, the Trust's historians, garden surveyors and archaeologists work together to interpret each property to discover its origins and development. By understanding each historic garden, conservation management is made possible.

The National Trust's Wessex Region (Somerset, Dorset, Wiltshire, Gloucestershire and the county that used to be Avon) contains a good selection of grand houses including architectural elements dating from the thirteenth to the twentieth centuries. This paper will briefly consider archaeological research that has taken place on four of these properties (Barrington Court and Montacute in Somerset, Lacock in Wiltshire and Dyrham in South Gloucestershire). It will conclude with a more detailed case study of Kingston Lacy in Dorset.

Recording at National Trust properties

Barrington Court

Barrington Court was the earliest mansion house to be acquired for the National Trust (1905). At the time of acquisition the house was in a poor state of repair. It had long been used as a farm house and cider store and many of the internal features had been lost. Despite

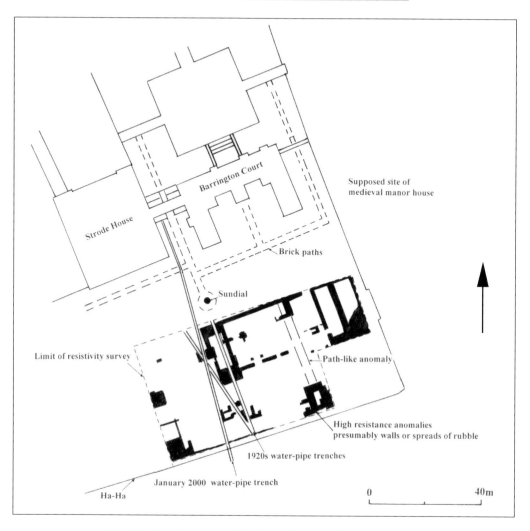

Fig. 6 Resistivity survey of the South Lawn at Barrington Court
(© National Trust)

this deterioration, the early sixteenth-century Hamstone exterior was still intact. However, the gardens for the house had become overgrown and forgotten.

In the 1920s Barrington was leased to the Lisle family who repaired the house and employed Gertrude Jekyll to design walled gardens on its west side. The main entrance was switched from the south to the north.

There were plans for elaborate garden designs for the East Orchard and South Lawn of the house but these were not implemented. This was fortunate because the East Orchard overlies the foundations of Barrington's medieval manor house and the South Lawn was found to contain evidence of sixteenth and seventeenth-century formal garden designs.

There are no pictures of the south front of the house and garden before 1839 (Fretwell 1992). The documentary evidence suggests that after the seventeenth century, the owners spent very little money on the property. Consequently, the south side of the house has been maintained as a lawn for over 250 years.

An opportunity to examine the buried archaeology arose when a new water pipe to the house was laid across the South Lawn in January 2000. This confirmed that very little recent work had been carried out to the garden. Beneath the turf were deposits containing seventeenth-century pottery and this material had been used to level the ground. Beneath the seventeenth century layers were the stone footings of a small building with a flagstone floor. The pottery from this building indicated a sixteenth-century date.

The evidence from the pipe trench and the open level nature of lawn encouraged local volunteers to use the Trust's geophysical equipment to survey the area. The results were processed in April 2001 and were extremely promising (Fig. 6). They have revealed a pattern of high resistance features indicating garden walls forming rectilinear borders parallel to and aligned with the walls of the house. The survey showed that the existing path from the central porch of the house once continued south and an area of high resistance across this linear feature may indicate the position of a gatehouse.

Montacute House

Slightly later than Barrington is its near neighbour Montacute House. This is also of golden Ham Hill sandstone and was completed by William Arnold in 1600 for the Phelips family. The boundaries of the formal Elizabethan gardens to the east and north survive. Their present layout can be recognised from a survey dating to 1667 (SRO DD/PH 226/16). The area of the north garden with its raised walks is much the same although its central prospect mound was replaced by a fountain in the nineteenth century.

The edging stones to the axial paths from the central fountain were replaced in 1998 and the narrow trenches were dug under archaeological supervision (Fig. 7). These revealed a narrow band of early seventeenth century garden soil but most of the older garden soils had been truncated by the elaborate garden bed designs of the later nineteenth century.

Like Barrington the principal entrance to the house had been changed. In the late eighteenth century the old road on the east side of Montacute House was diverted and a new entrance was constructed reusing masonry from the ruins of the nearby Clifton Maybank House.

On the east side of the house the 1667 survey reveals that originally a visitor would have left the old road, entered an outer walled court and then passed through a gatehouse between two pavilions. He would then have approached the house across an inner court, ascended a flight

Fig. 7 Excavation to replace path kerbs Montacute North Garden November 1998 (© National Trust)

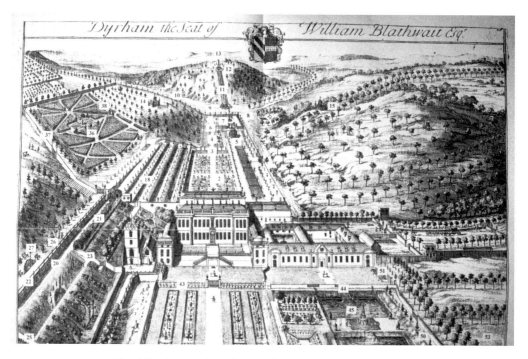

Fig. 8 Dyrham Park gardens as drawn by Johannes Kip 1712

of steps onto the east terrace before finally entering the house itself.

The terrace, the inner court and the pavilions survive but the gatehouse has been demolished and the outer court and road have gone. The earliest surviving map of Montacute by Samuel Donne dates to 1774 (SRO DD/PH 159). By that time the outer court and road had made way for a grand double avenue of trees that continued eastwards to the horizon.

In 1999 a resistivity survey detected the position of the old road and the path which branched from it to the house. Higher resistance features in the central area between the two pavilions were interpreted as indicating the possible site of the gatehouse. Four small evaluation trenches were excavated in March 2000 in advance of a proposed service trench. These revealed the buried garden soils of the outer east court but the only stonework found was a wall corner constructed of roughly dressed blocks of Ham stone. This stonework was thought to be too crudely made to be part of the gatehouse although it lay partly covered by the metalling of the central access track to the

house. The gatehouse is likely to have been as well built as the surviving pavilions that once flanked it. Further work is necessary and hopefully future research will enable details, recorded in the 1667 survey, such as the banqueting house and gatehouse, to be located.

Dyrham Park

Unlike Montacute, the original design of the garden at Dyrham can be visualised because of a detailed perspective view drawn by Johannes Kip in 1712 (Fig. 8). In the 1690s William Blathwayt, a courtier of William III, had commissioned a Dutch-style water garden to complement his new house. The water was piped from a reservoir at the top of the scarp slope down onto the floor of the natural amphitheatre in which Dyrham House was built. The water from the reservoir took several routes. The principal of these feeding a grand cascade flowing from a fountain decorated with a statue of Neptune. This was located on the scarp crest and from this point the water tumbled down a flight of steps into a large canal. Other channels of water fed fountains that occupied terraces on the north side of the garden. The intricate garden beds and many water features proved difficult to maintain and when they fell out of fashion the area was converted to a landscape park. By 1770 the east garden had been levelled and put down to grass.

Today the statue of Neptune, the north slope terraces and the reservoir are still visible but the rest of the garden lies under grass. Traces of the water garden can be seen as parch marks after dry weather.

The curators of the property have been tempted to try and recreate some of the details shown by Kip. However, overlaying Kip's view onto Ordnance Survey maps indicates that he enhanced his perspective and made the garden larger than life. A further obstacle to reconstruction is the archaeological evidence from geophysical survey.

Resistivity surveys of both the east and west gardens have revealed details not shown on the Kip drawing. The drawing has proved to be only a snapshot of a developing garden. The buried archaeology indicates a more complex picture. In August 1999, proposed drainage work in the east park necessitated the excavation of two evaluation trenches. These were located where the drain was to cross two high resistance anomalies. The north trench uncovered a stone filled pit 1m square and 1m deep and the south trench revealed a revetment wall, which was part of a raised garden which once flanked the canal.

Neither of these excavated features were anticipated from the Kip drawing and the archaeological results highlight the dangers of recreating historic gardens based solely on documentary sources.

Lacock Abbey

The earthworks of another abandoned water garden can be found in a meadow on the north side of Lacock Abbey. This was designed for John Ivory-Talbot in the early eighteenth century. Ivory-Talbot's notebooks reveal that he was often changing details of the garden. Many of the changes were implemented because it was difficult to keep the canals, leats and ponds full of water.

The water garden took advantage of the medieval mill stream and fish ponds constructed for the Augustinian nuns of Lacock Abbey. The abbey still has its thirteenth-century cloisters with many of the monastic rooms branching from them. These medieval features are surrounded by architectural additions dating from the sixteenth, eighteenth and nineteenth centuries.

The water garden is rectilinear in plan, its northern boundary is a leat created to divert the mill stream into the River Avon via a stone-lined cascade. Near this confluence, at the north-east corner of the old water garden, is a stone-faced bastion. Sluice gates could channel the flow of water around seven of the eight sides of the bastion and along a leat forming the east side of the garden. The bastion was designed as a viewing point and was subsequently selected as a site of strategic importance as in the 1940s a machine gun post was built on it. To balance the bastion, the garden designers created another feature at the north-west corner of the garden. This still survives and is known as the rockworks.

On its south-east side the rockworks takes the form of an arched cove, faced in tufa-like limestone. This was the side visible from the garden although care was also taken during the building of its north-east side. Here the rockworks has been constructed to resemble a romantic ruin. It is built of limestone rubble and brick. Below two string courses is an upper arch of limestone voussoirs apparently blocked with limestone rubble but with an open arch of voussoirs 1m below it. This lower arch once had water flowing through it but the stream was diverted in the late nineteenth century when the arch was blocked with soil and rubble.

A single photograph is known of this feature showing the water cascading under the arch. The Lacock Property Manager and garden staff would like this feature to be restored and archaeological excavations took place in May 1999 to determine the feasibility of reintroducing water through the arch (Fig. 9). The excavation uncovered the stone-lined water

Fig. 9 Excavation of the Lacock Rockworks arch May 1999
(© National Trust)

channel that directed the stream over a 0.8m high limestone step before the water flowed through the arch. The rockworks had been altered on more than one occasion but it seems to have been first constructed in the mid eighteenth century across an ancient stream channel. The lowest silts in the steam contained Romano-British pottery. A further season of work took place in June 2000 when the lower flagstone floor beneath the arch and sluice gate was uncovered. The masonry has now been consolidated for display to the public.

Kingston Lacy

Many National Trust houses are located on or near the remains of older buildings. Kingston Lacy is a good example of this. Visitors see a mansion first built in the seventeenth century with major alterations dating to the eighteenth and nineteenth centuries but there are records of an older house.

In August 1981 Henry John Ralph Bankes died and left his family estates of Kingston Lacy and Corfe Castle to the National Trust. The two estates lie 20 miles apart in south-east Dorset. The Corfe Castle Estate is a group of small Saxon manors purchased and united by Sir Christopher Hatton between 1572 and 1586.

Kingston Lacy is an 8,000 acre remnant of a great royal Saxon estate of over 30,000 acres (Fig. 10). In the 1630s Sir John Bankes purchased both estates and made the Castle of Corfe his family home. During the Civil War the Castle was besieged by parliamentary forces and was finally captured and sleighted in 1646.

In the 1660s, after the Restoration, John's son Sir Ralph Bankes decided to commission a new house, not at Corfe but at Kingston. Although there was no great house at Kingston there had once been a manor house there. The new house and park were created within the home farm of the estate at a place called 'Court Close'. There is no indication in the seventeenth-century documents that Sir Ralph knew that he chose a site close to the old house but the ruins may have been visible when the workmen arrived to dig the foundation trenches for the new mansion. Certainly, by the eighteenth century, the location of old Kingston Lacy had been forgotten. The historian Rev John Hutchins mentioned a rumour that Kingston Lacy was built on the site of a palace of the kings of Wessex but he could find no evidence of this.

In 1981, Mr Bankes not only gave the National Trust his land and buildings but also the Bankes family archive, a fine collection of documents. The earliest maps of the park are dated

Fig. 10 Aerial view of Kingston Lacey Park (© National Trust)

1742, 1774 and 1786. They describe the area north of the house as 'Court Close', a name suggestive of an old manor site and also recorded in the sixteenth century as a place name within the demesne farm of Kingston. The Tudor surveys list the land within Kingston Farm and record that the demesne farm contained the site of the manor.

The three eighteenth-century maps each show the east and west gardens with different details. Compared to the great land owners this was a modest park and garden, but throughout the eighteenth and nineteenth centuries additional blocks of the surrounding open fields of Kingston Lacy were enclosed to make the park larger. In 1742 a single north drive was shown leading from the house to the main road from Blandford to Wimborne. A statue was shown on the drive with a small classical temple sited on its east side. By 1774 a crows-foot design of drives converged on the north side of the house, the temple remained but the statue was not shown. To the south of the house was a walled Parterre Garden, divided by gravel paths into four lawns with a statue in each. To the east and west were two smaller compartments for evergreens, fruit trees and flowers. To the south of the lawns was a semicircular garden decorated with ten urns or statues. From this focal area, avenues of trees radiated out into the park. By 1786, many of the avenue trees had been

removed and the beds of the south garden were shown in a different design. By 1790, the park perimeter had been planted with a belt of beech trees and the formal gardens had been removed to create an open landscape park. In the early nineteenth century William John Bankes brought back an ancient Egyptian obelisk as a focal point for the south garden and soon afterwards other antiquarian stone carvings were brought to the garden from Italy and Egypt.

Despite all these previous garden overlays, today the garden and park are managed in the way Henrietta Bankes arranged them in the early 1900s. Although the most recent design of the garden is maintained the historical and archaeological research enables the traces of the earlier gardens and buildings to be recognised and conserved.

This outline of the known garden history leaves a number of questions. Of particular interest would be the discovery of the original garden design of the 1660s in relation to the position of medieval Kingston Lacy. There are also late seventeenth and early eighteenth-century references to an unlocated banqueting house that had been demolished by 1742.

In 1984, when Kingston Lacy House and park were being prepared for opening to the public, medieval pottery was unearthed when a lay-by was constructed on the north-east side of the house. Two years later a medieval building, known as Lodge Farm, on the north-west edge of Kingston Lacy Park was refurbished. The archaeological excavation and building recording there revealed it to be a fifteenth-century house. This stone building had been constructed over a backfilled ditch that contained medieval building rubble and also a deposit of fallow deer antlers. It was concluded that Lodge Farm had been the lodge for the park-keeper and forester of Kingston Lacy and had been constructed over a deer park boundary ditch near the site of an earlier hunting lodge. It was hoped that by looking at the Bankes Archive, references to the park-keeper's lodges might be found. The documents had been deposited at the Dorset Record Office and included 23 account rolls dating from 1380–1457. These medieval documents described Lodge Farm as Badbury Lodge within Badbury deer park but a surprise discovery was the mention of repairs to numerous other buildings. These repairs were recorded in a section of each parchment roll as 'expenses of the houses' and 'expenses of necessities'. Sarah Bridges, the archivist responsible for the Bankes family documents agreed to translate some of the account rolls. The size and complexity of the manorial buildings became apparent as the documents were transcribed. It was discovered that more of the account rolls survived at the Public Record Office. William Aird, an archivist at Dorchester, was employed to translate them. In addition to describing the building repairs they also described the location of the medieval garden within the Inner Court. They listed some of the plants growing there in the fourteenth century and included leeks, parsley, garlic and pear trees.

In January 1990, the great storm swept across Kingston Lacy Park and tore up many of the trees. One fell 150m north of the house and dragged up in its roots fragments of building rubble. The finds were similar to those found at Lodge Farm and included medieval pottery, glazed ceramic ridge tiles and Purbeck limestone

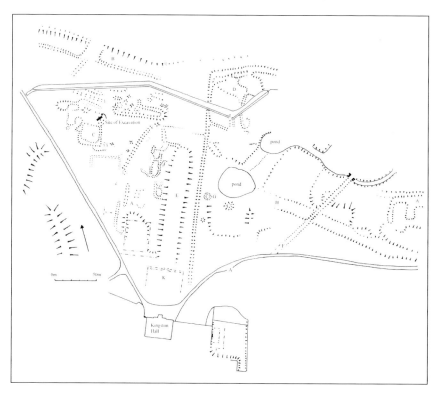

Fig. 11 Earthwork Survey of Kingston Lacy north park
(© National Trust)

roof tiles. The medieval account rolls record the purchase of thousands of stone tiles and the cost of transporting them from the Purbeck quarries to the manor.

In the spring of 1990, the north park was examined in detail and found to contain many earthworks (Fig. 11). Building rubble had been disturbed around a newly planted sapling and more building debris was discovered eroding from the cutting of a ha-ha, excavated in 1984 to keep Mr Bankes' Red Devon cattle visible but distant from visitors to the north park. The earthworks were surveyed and the survey plan indicated the position of a range of buildings overlain by eighteenth-century garden features.

In 1996, Geoffrey Brown volunteered to carry out a resistivity survey of the north park. The results of his work confirmed the findings of the earthwork survey and added details to the archaeological map of the site. The position of a house measuring 40m by 25m was pinpointed on the north-west side of the present Kingston Lacy House. The suspected wall footings of the medieval buildings, were overlaid by later garden features particularly the central embankment of the north drive shown on the 1742 map. The circular footings of the classical temple were also clear.

In May 1997 a small trench measuring 6m by 2m was excavated where the resistivity results had indicated the buried footings of the largest building. A 1m wide medieval wall was uncovered with floor surfaces dating to the fifteenth century. A robber trench cut into the wall contained pottery dating to the seventeenth century and suggests that the site was visible at that time.

Ralph Bankes' decision to site his new house near the old manor house and the position of the old house in relation to the new may have had significance in the original garden layout. The remains would have occupied the space west of the main entrance to the house. One could argue that the manor house feature was balanced by the ornamental ponds excavated on the east side of the drive. By the 1770s the medieval site and the ponds occupied the centres of triangles of ground surrounded by the drives of the crows-foot and the alignment of the Blandford to Wimborne Road. However, there are no records to confirm the assumption that Ralph Bankes sited his new house in relation to the old in such a considered way.

Conclusion

It is hoped that this selection of historic garden case studies will give an impression of the decision making and recording work taking place during necessary development within the gardens. In addition to this the report promotes the types of research undertaken by National Trust staff and volunteers both to understand and maintain these beautiful designed land-scapes.

References

Fretwell, K. 1988 'Montacute' National Trust Park and Garden Survey, unpublished internal report

Fretwell, K. 1992 'Barrington' National Trust Park and Garden Survey, unpub internal report

Kenworthy-Browne, J. 1999 *Dyrham Park* National Trust Guidebook

Papworth, M. 1998 'The Medieval Manorial Buildings of Kingston Lacy' *Proc. Dorset Natur. Hist. Archaeol. Soc.* 120, 42–62

Manuscript Sources in Somerset Record Office:
1667 Survey DD/PH 226/16
1782 Samuel Donne's Map

'Come, My Spade': Archaeology in Historic Gardens

Brian Dix

Come, my spade. There is no ancient gentlemen but gardeners, ditchers, and grave-makers; they hold up Adam's profession.

William Shakespeare, *Hamlet*, Act V, Scene 1.

Historic gardens exist in many forms. Some are wholly archaeological sites, while others retain a number of their earlier features; some have been accurately restored to a specific period but others are complete recreations, attempting to evoke an original spirit rather than being a faithful reconstruction.

Individual sites vary enormously in size, complexity and importance. They range in date from Roman to the twentieth century and, in addition to buried sites, extend from earthworks that once provided an ornamental setting for royal residences, castles and other great homes, to the lost features of modern public parks. They include surviving town and cottage gardens as well as the remains of the larger, often elaborate formal layouts that existed at country houses, where the wider surrounding of a designed landscape might contain parkland planting or have a picturesque quality created through carefully contrived scenes.

Although historical documents, maps and surveys may help to trace the development of houses and change in their settings, they frequently lack modern precision and innocently omit details that are central to the issues that most interest us today. The recognition of associated remains, extant in walls, surviving vegetation, and earthworks above ground or potentially preserved beneath the surface, holds a key to closer understanding. The proper examination of these archaeological remains, combined with the analysis of biological information and the interpretation of historical sources, reveals the extent and nature of places in the past and indicates their development through time.

It is now the commonplace for archaeological survey and related analysis to underpin bids for funding the repair and reuse of historic gardens and connected landscapes. Most importantly, by identifying areas of potential sensitivity and significance, the results from such investigation enable the consequences of proposed reconstruction and other change to be assessed, often highlighting the tension between preservation and enhancement.

Traces of long abandoned grounds and the gardens within them, together with the historic phases of those still in use, have been recorded since the end of the nineteenth century, when Alicia Amherst (1895, 86–7, 109–10, 116) identified fishponds, terraces and other relict features from earlier gardens. The growth of systematic survey by field archaeologists in the twentieth century, and in particular the work by Royal Commission investigators, led to an increasing identification of sites, especially from the 1960s onwards (Taylor 1991, 1–3). It is only since the 1980s, however, that the most important examples have received proper recognition in national records such as the *Register of Parks and Gardens of Special Historic Interest in England* (cf. English Heritage 1998).

There is a wealth of surviving field evidence (Taylor 1983. Cf. Brown 1991 and Pattison 1998, both *passim*). Early garden layouts, given up for reasons of economy, the lack of labour to maintain them, or simply a change of fashion, may be preserved beneath modern lawns. Together with the more prominent earthworks of mounts, terraces and canals, lesser scarps and hollows may denote the existence of former garden features, marking the lines of walls, fountain basins, raised walks and other paths. Evidence of large-scale earthmoving for previous landscape effect might be indicated by mottled crop-marks and pitting visible in air photographs or traceable on the ground through different grasses or changes of vegetation.

The careful observation and analysis of the shapes and layout of features and variation within them can lead to the discovery of old flowerbeds, as well as former boundaries and other enclosing features. Similarly, earlier tree-sites may be discernible from the hollows caused by removal of their trunks or through distinctive vegetation encouraged by the higher levels of fertility within the zone of rotted root-material. Studying the species, form and branch structure of any surviving trees and bushes can give evidence of past function and use, as well as suggesting dates of planting (Rackham 1990, 4–18. Cf. Pigott 1995). Important details are

also revealed by analysing the relationship of trees to other aspects of the natural and man-made landscape, which can show how the existing landform influenced development or was indeed changed by it.

Geophysical survey techniques may help to define more accurately the nature and pattern of chronological and spatial variation. On suitable geology, magnetometry and electrical earth resistance measurement, or resistivity, can reveal traces of buried paths and flowerbeds, as well as locating garden walls and ornamental features (Cole *et al.* 1997). The lost elements of successive phases of a garden's history may often be identified but, like other non-intrusive surveys, the detail of their evolution can only be understood with the aid of the historical record and through related archaeological excavation.

The scope of excavation ranges from the comprehensive to the selective, targeting particular aspects either for the academic interest of the historical information alone, or for assessing the veracity of a reconstruction. Thus, the investigation may be used to gather detailed information concerning site history and development, defining the appearance at specific times, as well as to test the degree of survival of the buried layout to ensure that significant features are not lost or obscured during routine maintenance or repair. Sampling strategies might therefore range from uncovering an entire formal garden in readiness for accurate reconstruction to the examination of the salient points and key features of the grounds (Dix 1999, 370–2).

Traces of plants associated with old garden features may be preserved in the soil. They can include seeds, pollen and phytoliths, as well as larger remains such as leaves, stems, wood and roots. With the remains of molluscs, insects and vertebrates, such botanical information can improve knowledge of the former environment and supplement historical planting records. Related soil microfabric analysis and chemistry may show the extent and nature of deliberate enrichment or other improvement, further indicating the original gardening practice (Currie and Locock 1991; de Moulins and Weir 1997).

Archaeological excavation enables us to identify the original methods of ground preparation and the nature of building materials. Reconstructing former earth profiles becomes possible and the setting of paths and major architectural features are revealed, together with the accurate location of earlier tree-pits and other planting arrangements. The excavation of paths, for example, can provide evidence for the material of their construction as well as the details of their former dimensions, previous cross-section and original layout. The historic form of individual features, including grottoes and fountains, as well as mounts and terraces can also be discovered (cf. Dix *et al.* 1995).

Depending upon the condition of its preservation, the garden plan may be recoverable. Its reconstruction on the basis of the excavated ground plan would thus match the exact dimensions and layout of the original features. Likewise, the position of flowerbeds and paths, together with the location of architectural work and other landscaping, would be faithful to the original design and follow precisely the alignment and relative height of the former features as denoted by archaeological excavation. The use of identical or similar materials to those that were originally employed would add to the authentic setting.

Early recreations of former gardens owed more to art-historical study and contemporary horticultural design than to archaeological research, which only began on historic sites in the 1930s following the example of work in ancient Roman gardens (Dix 1999, 368–9). Then, the results from excavating along previous walls and uncovering former paths and steps were used as the basis for reconstruction at several sites on both sides of the Atlantic. It is only more recently, in work undertaken since 1970 and in particular from about 1985 onwards, that flowerbeds and a more complete range of evidence have begun to be examined (Taylor 1991, 3–4. Cf. Kelso and Most 1990). The majority of such investigation has been connected with the reinstatement of the basic architectural form of an individual garden, thereby favouring sites that date from when a formal layout was fashionable. Among them, the reconstruction of King William III's Privy

Garden at Hampton Court may be reckoned a landmark in achievement and successfully restores the harmony that was always intended to exist with the palace (Thurley 1995).

The relationship between built and landscaped forms, with the appropriate analysis of the connection between space and sight, enables us to approach the original concept of design and visual planning. Archaeological field survey and excavation provide the means to discover specific details of previous layout and planting, showing how historic gardens and associated landscapes were built, maintained, and developed. Through the results, we can enter into the time and the mind of the original owners and designers. The effect is to rediscover the spirit of the place.

References

Amherst, A. 1895 *A History of Gardening in England*

Brown, A. E. (ed.) 1991 *Garden Archaeology* Council for British Archaeology Research Report No. 78

Cole, M. A., David, A. U. E., Linford, N. T., Linford, P. K. and Payne, A. W. 1997 Non-destructive techniques in English gardens: geophysical prospecting, in Jacques 1997, 26–39

Currie, C. K. and Locock, M. 1991 An evaluation of archaeological techniques used at Castle Bromwich Hall, 1989–90, *Garden History*, 19.1, 77–99

de Moulins, D. and Weir, D. A. 1997 The potential and use of environmental techniques in gardens, in Jacques 1997, 40–46

Dix, B. 1999 'Of Cabbages – and Kings': Garden Archaeology in Action, in G. Egan and R. L. Michael, eds, *Old and New Worlds. Historical/ Post Medieval Archaeology Papers from the Societies' joint conferences at Williamsburg and London 1997 to mark thirty years of work and achievement*, 368–77

Dix, B., Soden, I. and Hylton, T. 1995 Kirby Hall and its gardens: excavations in 1987–1994, *Archaeological Journal*, 152, 291–380

English Heritage 1998 *The Register of Parks and Gardens. An introduction*

Jacques, D. (ed.) 1997 *The Techniques and Uses of Garden Archaeology, Journal of Garden History*, 17.1

Kelso, W. M. and Most, R. (eds) 1990 *Earth Patterns. Essays in Landscape Archaeology*, Charlottesville and London: University Press of Virginia

Pattison, P. (ed.) 1998 *There by Design. Field Archaeology in Parks and Gardens*, Royal Commission on the Historical Monuments of England

Pigott, D. 1995 The radial growth rate of yews (Taxus baccata) at Hampton Court, Middlesex,

Garden History, 23.2, 249–52

Rackham, O. 1990 *Trees and Woodland in the British Landscape*, 2nd edn J. M. Dent

Taylor, C. 1983 *The Archaeology of Gardens*

Taylor, C. C. 1991 Garden archaeology: an introduction, in Brown 1991, 1–5

Thurley, S. (ed.) 1995 *The King's Privy Garden at Hampton Court Palace 1689–1995*, London: Apollo Magazine

Medieval Gardens and Designed Landscapes

Paul Everson

Introduction

Any introduction to designed landscapes needs to take into account the evidence of medieval gardens. Hitherto this subject has been approached through documentary, literary and art historical sources (as, for example, Harvey 1981; McLean 1981), but more recently there has been a significant contribution made by archaeologists, led by Chris Taylor (for example, Taylor 2000; Everson 1998).

The patchy nature of archaeological work in this subject means that compelling examples exist only outside the South West. But, the approaches deployed elsewhere, and illustrated here, exhibit the right methodology: the rigorous study of the field remains that are the legitimate source material, and a proper awareness of the intimate interrelationship between the residence and the garden or designed landscape that provided its setting. I emphasise this intimate relationship as one too easily overlooked in discussing gardens, and offer the useful generic or overarching characterisation – which I think I had from Christopher Taylor – of gardens as 'the pleasurable elaboration of the setting of well-to-do residences' (English Heritage 1997, 2).

Medieval Gardens

In Thomas Malory's *Morte d'Arthur*, Sir Launcelot in his madness is discovered sleeping in the garden of her father's palace by the Lady

Elaine. Attendant ladies who are dancing or dallying are dismissed and the knight is taken into her care for cure by religious powers. Insofar as the *hortus conclusus* or herber is thought of as the characteristic form of medieval gardens, with its literary context in the rituals of courtly love and religious symbolism, archaeologists have struggled to identify clear-cut examples either in excavation or in fieldwork.

An excavated layout at Haverfordwest Priory (Rees 1996) has apparently confirmed in scale and detailing some of the presumptions that underpin a number of modern re-creations (cf. Landsberg 1996, 101–30). Earthworks at St Cross Hospital at Winchester, founded in 1136 but with the standing fabric of the hospital ranges dating from the mid fifteenth century, have been interpreted in terms of a medieval

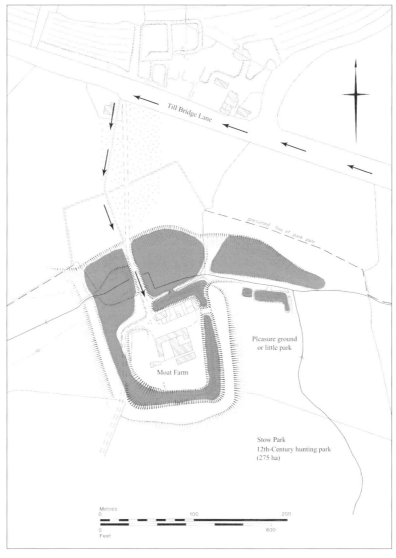

Fig. 12 The bishop of Lincoln's palace and hunting park at Stow Park, Lincolnshire: simplified interpretation diagram, after Everson et al 1991, fig. 130 – 'delightfully surrounded with woods and ponds' (© Crown copyright. NMR)

garden layout (Currie 1992): and recent work by Christopher Taylor and co-workers at Bassingbourn in Cambridgeshire has identified others (Oosthuizen and Taylor 2000a; 2000b). But the fourteenth-century garden within one corner of the curtilage of the former bishop's palace at Nettleham in Lincolnshire, which is simply structured with low terraces and intimately integrated with the residential ranges of the palace, probably remains the most reliable and securely dated example we know archaeologically (Everson *et al* 1991, 129–31); though it is matched in form and integration with the residential ranges – but far exceeded in scale – by the earthworks of the royal gardens at Clarendon Palace in Wiltshire (see RCHME survey by Nicky Smith and Jo Donahie in NMR, archive item 928586).

The same programme of fieldwork in Lincolnshire that recorded Nettlesham, set us off on an alternative, complementary trail in the understanding of the designed setting of major medieval residences. It began with another palace of the bishops of Lincoln, at their great hunting park at Stow Park 10 miles north west of Lincoln. Here the oblique approach to the residence along the Roman road afforded an unfolding view of it across a shallow valley: then access was head on, through an outer enclosure, and across a causeway between extensive sheets of water dammed in the valley (Fig. 12; Everson *et al* 1991, 184–5). The aesthetic quality of the experience created – 'delightfully surrounded with woods and ponds' – was noted by the twelfth-century hagiographer, Giraldus Cambrensis, even though the prime point of his account was the symbolism of the swans present on the ponds and of their actions. This surely is a designed landscape of twelfth-century origin, combining a managed approach, deployment of water features – to surround, to reflect, to support fish and birds that carry their own symbolism – probably an enclosed garden or pleasure ground adjacent to the residence, and the backdrop of a wooded hunting park. Other rural episcopal and archiepiscopal palaces around the country have proved to be endowed with designed adjuncts when viewed in this way – Somersham in Cambridgeshire (Taylor 1989), Cawood near York (Blood and Taylor 1992),

Alvechurch in Worcestershire (Aston 1970–72), Bishops Waltham in Hampshire (Hare 1988), or Buckden near Peterborough (RCHM(E) 1926, 34–8, 40). An example like Sées in lower Normandy argues that these creations had a wider currency. There, a rectangular plot of land attached to the episcopal palace – similar to Buckden's 'Little Park' – is surrounded by water channels diverted from the river Orne and affords stunning views of the cathedral – an ever-present reminder of the occupant's commitment and inspiration. Indeed, some of the contemporary accounts most relevant to this reading of English field remains lie in French documentary sources (for example, Van Buren 1986).

Medieval Secular Designed Landscapes

The same concerns and creations are found with major secular medieval residences, but generally writ larger. Bodiam Castle in Sussex, built by Sir Edward Dallingridge in 1385, remains one of the most striking and accessible instances (Taylor *et al* 1990; Everson 1996). That site's embodiment of structured – almost ritualised – routes of access finds its clearest literary expression, as David Austin has noted in discussing Barnard Castle (in a lecture at Oxford, February 2001), in the proper comportment of a true knight such as Sir Gawain in the fourteenth century poetic romance, in contrast to the behaviour of his rival the Green Knight that ignores all such forms and structures. The proper treatment of arriving guests exhibits a similar formality and graduated care, that imbued lordly society and permeates its literary and artistic portrayal (Girouard 1978, 64).

The case study that Bodiam comprises has generated an impression that manipulation of water was an essential and invariable concomitant of medieval designed landscapes – even to use of the terms 'water castle' or 'fantasy castle'. Certainly, taking it as a convenient identifying feature many candidates for this manner

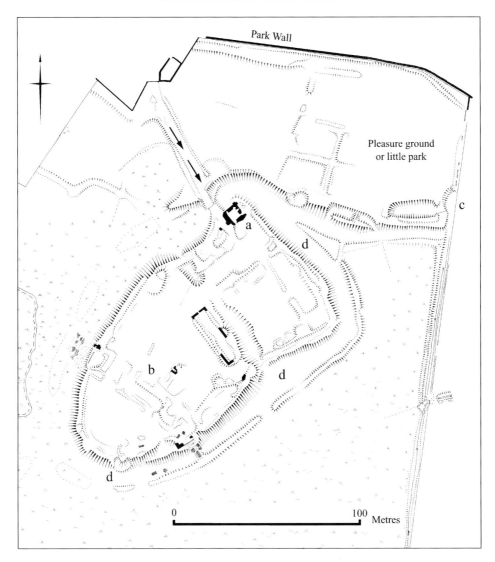

Fig. 13 Ravensworth Castle, North Yorkshire. Plan based on RCHME survey in 1997 –
(a) gatehouse, (b) site of chapel, (c) spring, (d) 'moat'. (© Crown copyright. NMR)

of understanding can be named. They include the great and well-known, such as Kenilworth, Leeds, Bolingbroke and Framlingham (to name just the four discussed and illustrated in Taylor 1998); but also by comparison obscure, largely earthwork survivals, including Pan Castle near Whitchurch in Shropshire (NMR no. SJ 54 SW 12), Shotwick Castle in Cheshire, or Whorlton Castle in North Yorkshire (Everson 1998). Detailed field survey is commonly necessary in order to engage with an understanding of such

sites, though not often to record them for the first time as new discoveries – since most are already logged in national and local archaeological records even if misidentified or misunderstood – nor even necessarily to add large amounts of additional details, though that is frequently possible. Rather, the process is often one of working through an altered focus of perception, seeking insight in interpretation and understanding rather than solely describing or pigeon-holing. It is also a process of showing

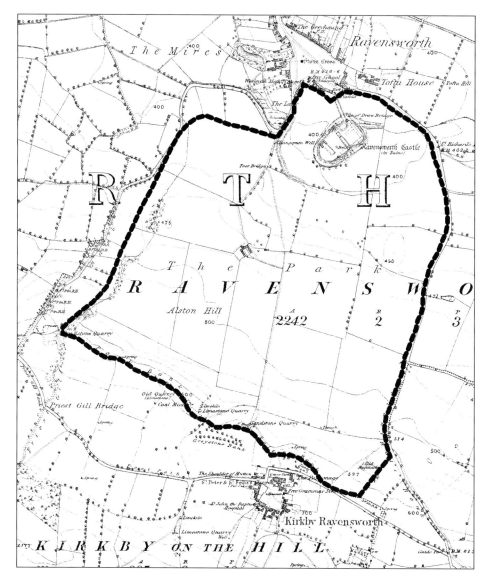

*Fig. 14 Ravensworth Castle, North Yorkshire. Plan of park,
based on Ordnance Survey 1st ed. 6" map*

an awareness of context, which is suggested, confirmed or reinforced by accumulative detail within the field remains.

The site of Ravensworth Castle in Richmondshire may serve to illustrate this (Lofthouse 1997; NMR no. NZ 10 NW 1). Briefly, Ravensworth was the seat of the Fitzhugh family throughout the Middle Ages until the estate was split up for lack of a direct male heir in 1512. The family was ennobled in the late fourteenth century. It may be a significant conjunction that Henry Fitzhugh II was granted a licence in 1391 to enclose 200 acres around the castle as a park or to extend an existing park and that the surviving ruined buildings suggest a thorough rebuilding of that same date. Those buildings, forming the core residence, occupy what is effectively an island within a large shallow, valley-bottom mere lying principally to the south (Fig. 13). That island was artificially created, through major efforts of earthmoving, out of what had apparently formerly been a spur of higher ground sticking out into the valley bottom. This was done in such a way that a narrow water-filled moat, fed from a spring, would remain around the island even should the mere suffer from seasonal drying out. Perhaps the embankment of the moat, though now fragmented, also formed a walk – outside the curtain and, as it were, on the water. Access to the site was through the walled park pale, via a straight way and causeway or bridge, head on to an imposing gatehouse embellished with emblems of castle architecture such as thin stepped corner buttresses and cruciform arrow slits. What remains of a south-west tower also incorporates a gun loop, more relevant to show than effect. Large windows even at ground floor level and a low, thin curtain wall further indicate the priority of aesthetics and show over any notional considerations of serious defence. The area of 'mainland' within the pale and adjacent to the access bears traces of subdivision, rectangular plots and small ponds, and may have been a form of pleasure ground or 'little park' (Taylor 2000, fig. 2: cf. Landsberg 1996; Everson 1998). The attached hunting park of something over 100ha (250 acres) extends up the hill to the south, up to but not encompassing the ancient church of Kirby Hill, which forms a feature on the skyline from the castle (Fig. 14). Views both from the top of the park and from the approach road over the hills from Richmond must have presented a scene to match that from the viewing platform or pleasaunce at Bodiam.

Here, surely, is a created landscape setting, contrived for pleasure and visual impact, for a major residence that itself was cast in a castellar garb. It is arguably a close contemporary of Bodiam, created in the last quarter of the fourteenth century. The prominent architectural inscription asserting 'Christus dominus Ihesus, via fons et origo, alpha et omega' which formerly encircled the third stage of the chapel's belfry tower is a reminder that that setting itself may have carried or incorporated deep-rooted symbolic and religious meaning, difficult though it is for us to recognise it archaeologically. At the least, a natural bog or mere watched over prominently by an early Christian site like Kirby Hill might suggest the conversion of a location of ancient ritual significance (Stocker and Everson 2003). Perhaps, even, the castle itself re-occupied a key, focal location – a promontory extending into the valley floor – and deliberately arrogated or adopted the authority imbued in it.

Ravensworth may appear geographically distant from the perspective of an audience in south west England. If nothing else, however, it demonstrates that the phenomenon of medieval designed landscapes is not confined to the south east and the metropolitan fringe, and was not excluded from regions sometimes characterised as lawless or at least of local independence of mind. Indeed it may prove to be the pasture areas of the north and west where the best survival of field evidence will occur.

Though I am aware that relevant work is in hand at Godolphin, for example (Herring 1998), the nearest I can come to a Westcountry example based on new detailed fieldwork is Ludgershall Castle in Wiltshire (Everson *et al* 2000). This example allows me to assert that these are not 'fantasy' castles in any sense of being trivial or not being castles in contemporary terms – far from it (Stocker 1993). It also permits me to demonstrate that water was not an invariable part of every medieval designed landscape.

Ludgershall was a royal castle. Its plan has traditionally been interpreted as a ringwork and bailey, and been cast in a military mode with its creation related to the civil war of Stephen and Matilda. Excavations in the 1960s and 1970s investigated it within that framework of thought. Field survey of the earthworks and consideration of the topographical context written up to support publication of those excavations have perceived it in a different way. This new interpretation proposes that the sub-oval bailey is in fact a pre-existing hillfort, over the northern end of which the medieval castle enclosure was superimposed. It notes that the enclosure itself and the layout of buildings within it are formally designed and remarkably regular. The enclosure is symmetrical, perhaps even polygonal: its form of double bank and ditch echoes that of the fort: its circuit is divided equally into three stretches of different physical form. It appears to be divided internally into three compartments matching the differences in circuit: the excavated one of these is devoted exclusively to the royal residential apartments: the great hall stood centrally in this arrangement, on an east-west orientation. There were arguably two opposed entrances in the form of a lost gatehouse located centrally in the south sector and a way out north into the park, marked by a gap in the circuit. Most distinctively, the north-east sector is a wide, flat-topped terrace – a walk or raised garden – that complements the residential apartments and was linked architecturally to them.

Furthermore, the royal castle had two parks associated with it, together occupying much of the parish of Ludgershall. One lay detached to the south-east, but the other lay along the northern side of the castle, and was subtly located to achieve maximum integration with it. Both the raised garden and the stack of residential chambers in the form of a tower – *aka* 'keep'

– looked out into this park, which thereby formed a theatre for staging hunting events within a landscape that was richly allusive.

There may be a debate whether what we see now was the original late twelfth-century creation as a royal residence, or whether it took over and reworked a 'military' ringwork of mid twelfth-century date. But if the latter, the adaptation was in place by about 1200, and would represent a remarkable – perhaps an implausibly remarkable – act.

In our age of sound-bites, then, Ludgershall is 'BODIAM WITHOUT WATER'. Thus Christopher Taylor urges me to describe it, so that people understand and take notice of what we are identifying here, and register the innovation of the perception being made.

There are certainly other examples, albeit not yet perceived, and many of them. For the point here is not the catalogue of specific examples that have been worked on, pointed to or guessed at, which I may be able to parade on this or any other occasion. Rather, the crucial point is

Fig. 15 Nunney Castle and village, Somerset: aerial view from the south. (© West Air Photography, Weston-Super-Mare; ref. Y 678 10)

the acceptance of the presumption that these great medieval residences of royalty, secular lords and prelates would routinely – invariably – have been supported by manipulated, designed landscapes involving careful forethought, planning, effort and cost not dissimilar to those attending designed landscapes of later eras. And the acknowledgement that, in favourable circumstances, their archaeological traces are there to be discerned and interpreted, if one can look with open, inquisitive eyes, attuned to issues of purpose, meaning and context.

So, in the south-western counties – despite a relative absence of archaeological activity directed at this topic – I should expect there to be the potential for new understanding about the designed landscape setting of such obvious late medieval candidates as the castles at Farleigh Hungerford in Wiltshire and Nunney in Somerset. At Nunney, for example, the strangely limited moated context of the tall, and architecturally distinctive, fourteenth-century residential block may originate in an arrangement similar to that at Ravensworth (Fig. 15). That is, a substantial mere filling the valley bottom and a

Fig. 16 Holwell Castle, Parracombe, Devon: aerial view from the north
(NMR SS 6644/32; © Crown copyright. NMR)

'moat' within it outlining the residence itself in a permanently secured ring of water. The church of All Saints is located on the valley side, clearly above the SE edge of the conjectured mere (as formerly was the early cross now re-sited in Church Street): a rectangular earthwork platform on rising ground to the north west, which has been categorised as an ornamental feature (Ordnance Survey Record Card ST 47 NW 6), may be a candidate for a pleasaunce. The conjecture would mean that much of the present core of Nunney village had developed latterly within the limits of the former mere. To judge from the Listed Building Lists (DoE 1984) the present properties in Church Street and Castle Street date only from the mid eighteenth-century onwards, whereas earlier buildings, such as Court Farmhouse, are set back higher on the slope. It surely is not irrelevant that the residential lords and builders of the castle, whose imposing monuments of fourteenth and early fifteenth century date occupy the north transept of All Saints church, bore the surname 'de la Mere' (MPBW 1956; Pevsner 1958).

The issues sketched out here ought to be relevant in the case of such great residences further west as Corfe or Restormel (see Herring, this volume) or Okehampton. This is especially so in the latter instance because of its almost complete re-creation in *c.*1300 as a grand residence, and the contemporary development of its great hunting park (Austin *et al* 1980; Higham *et al* 1982). Even for so archetypical a motte-and-bailey castle as Holwell in Parracombe in the western part of Exmoor (Fig. 16), it is clear on the ground that it sat within a buffer zone of closes watered by the two confluent streams, in relation to which access was negotiated. Some consideration of how it is positioned in the landscape, how access worked, and how that interrelated with its immediate surroundings would undoubtedly reveal deliberate decisions about location and setting that are to do with the appurtenances and projection of lordship rather than narrowly military considerations.

Acknowledgements

Thanks are due to Deborah Cunliffe who drew the illustrations.

References

Aston, M.A. 1970–72 'Earthworks at the Bishop's Palace, Alvechurch, Worcestershire', *Trans. Worcestershire Archaeol. Soc.* 3 ser., 3, 55–60

Austin, D., Daggett, R.H., and Walker M.J.C. 1980 'Farms and fields in Okehampton Park, Devon', *Landscape History* 2, 39–57

Blood, N.K. and Taylor, C.C. 1991 'Cawood, an archiepiscopal landscape', *Yorkshire Archaeol. J.*, 64, 83–102

Currie, C. 1992 'St Cross: a medieval moated garden?', *Journal of the Hampshire Gardens Trust* 11, 19–22

DoE 1984 *List of Listed Buildings, District of Mendip, Somerset*

English Heritage 1997 *Post-medieval Formal Gardens*, Single Monument Class Description for the Monuments Protection Programme of English Heritage

Everson, P. 1996 'Bodiam Castle, East Sussex: castle and its designed landscape', *Château Gaillard: études de castellologie médiévale* XVII, 79–84

Everson, P. 1998 '"Delightfully surrounded with woods and ponds": field evidence for medieval gardens in England', in P. Pattison (ed.), *There by design*, RCHME and British Archaeological Reports British Series, 267, 32–8

Everson, P., Brown, G. and Stocker, D. 2000 'The castle earthworks and landscape context', in P. Ellis (ed.), *Ludgershall Castle, Wiltshire: a report on the excavations by Peter Addyman, 1964–1972*, Wiltshire Archaeological and Natural History Society Monograph Series 2, 97–120

Everson, P., Taylor C.C. and Dunn, C.J. 1991 *Change and Continuity: rural settlement in north-west Lincolnshire*

Girouard, M. 1978 *Life in the English Country House*, Yale: New Haven and London

Hare, J.N. 1988 'Bishops Waltham Palace, Hampshire: William Wykeham, Henry Beaufort and the transformation of a medieval episcopal palace', *Archaeol. J.* 145, 222–54

Harvey, J. 1981 *Medieval Gardens*

Herring, P. 1998 *Godolphin, Breage. An archaeological and historical assessment*, Cornwall Archaeological Unit, Truro

Higham, R.A., Allan, J.P. and Blaylock, S.R. 1982 'Excavations at Okehampton Castle: Part 2: the Bailey', *Proc. Devon Archaeol. Soc.* 40, 19–152

Landsberg, S. 1996 *The Medieval Garden*

Lofthouse, C. 1997 'Ravensworth Castle and environs, Yorkshire', unpub RCHME site report deposited in NMR, NZ 10 NW 1

McLean, T. 1981 *Medieval English Gardens*

MPBW 1956 *Nunney Castle, blue guide*

Oosthuizen, S.M. and Taylor, C.C. 2000a 'Rediscovery of a vanished garden in Bassingbourn, Cambridgeshire, and the impact of the Lynne family on the medieval landscape', *Proc. Cambridge Antiq. Soc.* 139, 59–68

Oosthuizen, S.M. and Taylor, C.C. 2000b 'John O'Gaunt's House, Bassingbourn, Cambridgeshire: a fifteenth-century garden and landscape', *Landscape History* 22, 61–76

Pevsner, N. 1958 *Buildings of England. Somerset: South and West*

Rees, S. 1996 'The secret garden', *Heritage in Wales* 6, 11–13

Royal Commission on Historical Monuments (England) 1926 *An Inventory of the Historical Monuments in Huntingdonshire*

Stocker, D. 1993 'The shadow of the general's armchair', *Archaeol. J.*, 149, 415–20

Stocker, D. and Everson, P. 2003 'The straight and narrow way; fenland causeways and the conversion of the landscape in the Witham valley, Lincolnshire', in M. Carver (ed.), *The Cross goes North. Processes of Conversion on Northern Europe AD 300–1300*, 271–88

Taylor, C.C. 1989 'Somersham Palace, Cambridgeshire: a medieval landscape for pleasure?', in M. Bowden, D. Mackay and P. Topping (eds.), *From Cornwall to Caithness, British Archaeological Reports British Series*, 209, 211–24

Taylor, C.C. 1998 'From record to recognition; the discovery and understanding of the remains of parks and gardens', in P. Pattison (ed.), *There by design*, RCHME and British Archaeological Reports British Series, 267, 1–6

Taylor, C.C. 2000 'Medieval ornamental landscapes', *Landscapes* 1 no. 1, 38–55

Taylor, C.C., Everson, P. and Wilson-North, R. 1990 'Bodiam Castle, Sussex', *Medieval Archaeol.*, 34, 155–7

Van Buren, A.H. 1986 'Reality and literary romance in the park of Hesdin', in E.B. MacDougall, *Dumbarton Oaks Colloquium in the History of Landscape Architecture* 9, 117–34

Cornish Medieval Deer Parks

Peter Herring

Introduction

Cornwall's medieval deer parks have long been overlooked by most historians and archaeologists. Parks were among the earliest truly restricted outdoor spaces, keeping people out as much as keeping deer in and as such, closer study of them tells us more than that lords enjoyed hunting and ate and gave venison to signify their status (cf. Platt 1978, 47; Cantor 1982, 77). They give insights into wider historical issues.

In Cambridgeshire, Twigs Way (1997) has illustrated meaningful correlations between medieval and post-medieval parks and significant elements of contemporary social landscapes: manorial settlements, churches, and the typically nucleated settlements of that part of Britain. She showed how parks made unequal power relations concrete and permanently visible. For example, they enabled lords to separate themselves and their pleasure from the rest of local society, often at the expense of their tenants' previously held communal rights. Sometimes lords reinforced their social position by associating themselves through their parks with other symbols of local power, like the church. Elsewhere lords can be seen wholly or partially removing existing settlements and field systems to make way for parks, and significantly constraining the development of other settlements. It will be seen that there were similar arrangements or events in medieval Cornish parks, which are revealing of contemporary Cornish society.

By being imposed on the relatively open medieval landscape and thus physically altering the arena of medieval rural life, early parks are likely to have stimulated further social, landscape and architectural change. In Cornwall at least, the parks also demonstrate the application of landscape design that not only helped secure their creators' political aims, whether overt or otherwise, but also celebrated the aesthetic qualities of the landscape and the excitement of the pursuit of deer. Medieval deer parks were as carefully designed as early modern landscape parks; positioned and shaped and provided with entrances, pathways and views to not only represent certain socio-political aims but also to achieve sophisticated aesthetic effects, akin in many ways to those identified in later medieval gardens (Everson 1998; Everson and Williamson 1998).

Previous Work, Chronology and Sources

Early topographers listed extant and remembered Cornish deer parks: from Norden (in the 1580s), through Carew (1602), Tonkin (1730s) and Borlase (1750s), to Drew, Gilbert and Lysons in the early nineteenth century. More detailed research was undertaken by Shirley (1867) and by Charles Henderson in *c*.1928 (Henderson nd), and a good recent collation of all these sources was made by Douglas Ellory Pett in his work on Cornish parks and gardens (1998).

Cornwall Sites and Monuments Record includes records of other deer parks, some gleaned from local antiquarian research and others from field-names in early Victorian Tithe Awards. (NB In Cornwall, the field-name Park was 'the normal word for an enclosed field' (Padel 1985, 175) and cannot be used to suggest the former existence of a park (cf. Way 1997); only field-names containing the phrase Deer Park have been included.) Other parks have been found during this study among published national rolls, including those collated by Cantor (1983) and Way (1997). There are very few Cornish licences for empaling; most early deer parks were first recorded only when they were broken into.

These sources give a total of 123 pre-twentieth century Cornish deer parks identified to date and the number will no doubt continue to grow as research continues (see postscript). Of these, 49 can certainly be dated to before 1550, another 26 probably so; 48 are definitely

post-medieval. It is worth noting that many parks are likely to have been created significantly earlier than their first appearance in the surviving records; Hoppitt (2000) suggests that Suffolk deer parks were created an average of 75–80 years before the earliest surviving reference. Twelve Cornish deer parks are known to have been extant by the end of the thirteenth century, and there were probably more. Although not securely documented, several parks may be earlier. The three parks created by the Cardinan family at Restormel, Cardinham (Kenketh/Pinsla), and Penhallam could belong to the later twelfth century (see below). We have, then, an imprecise chronology for Cornish deer parks, but a chronological distinction between medieval and later parks may itself be less meaningful than once thought, those of the earlier period performing many of the same functions as those of the eighteenth century (Way 1997).

Although none is securely documented to before 1250, several Cornish parks are almost certainly earlier than the thirteenth century. It is unlikely, however, that there were very many pre-1204 parks in Cornwall as Forest Law had been applied to the whole county at some unknown time during the reign of Henry II (1154–89) (Bond 1994, 123). It is therefore doubtful that the king would have tolerated private parks co-existing with his Forest (unless they belonged either to favourites or particularly important families). Most of Cornwall was disafforested in return for heavy payments to King John in 1204, while the remainder, Foweymore (now Bodmin Moor), followed in 1214 (*ibid.*).

The Cornwall Archaeological Unit has carried out several detailed field surveys of deer parks, notably Godolphin, Lanhydrock, Carn Brea and Pengersick (Herring 1997; Thomas 1998; Herring *et al* 1998), as much for the well-preserved earlier features protected within their pales as for the parks themselves (see also Brown 1998). In fact there has been little in the way of analysis and interpretation of Cornish deer parks. This paper seeks to initiate closer study of Cornwall's parks by placing them in their contemporary landscape and considering their landscape design, principally by looking at the use their creators made of natural and earlier and contemporary cultural features. A number of parks have been briefly inspected for this paper. It is hoped that the results prove sufficiently interesting to stimulate more detailed research.

Distribution, Locations, Forms of Landscape Enclosed and Sizes of Parks

Most early Cornish parks can be identified in the landscape: through place, field and wood names or surviving lengths of boundary. These were mainly banks, probably originally with hedges or pales along their tops, all with internal ditches, and some, like Godolphin, with stone

facing. Only for about twenty of the medieval Cornish parks is it possible to reconstruct their shapes with any confidence. Deer parks of the Earldom of Cornwall and then from 1337 the Duchy of Cornwall are among the best documented and best defined. Most of these were in use for over 250 years and roads and field systems developed in relation to them. The parks of principal families often had shorter lives and some seem to have had several phases of expansion and retraction, leaving more complex and less easily discernible shapes.

The known medieval deer parks are unevenly distributed across Cornwall, with most in the eastern half of the county. All Earldom/Duchy deer parks are east of the Fowey/Camel line although the estate held just as much land to the west of it. This may reflect a preference for the more wooded parts of the region, a pattern that has been observed in many parts of England (Cantor 1982, 78–9), but in Cornwall it also

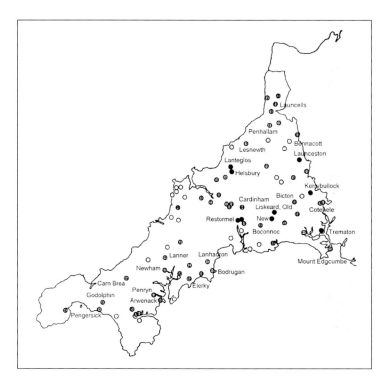

Fig. 17 Distribution of medieval deer parks in Cornwall, locating those mentioned in the text. Earldom/Duchy of Cornwall parks shown solid, other certainly medieval parks shaded, and other possible medieval parks open (© Peter Herring)

echoes the distribution of medieval castles, in part reflecting relationships between some castles and parks (see below). Less immediately obvious is a bias away from upland rough ground, though those parks that are partly in downland, like Carn Brea, Godolphin, and Kerrybullock, are among the best preserved, and have received most archaeological attention. Contrary to the traditional view of the deer park situated for economic reasons on poorer quality land (e.g. Cantor 1983, 3), most Cornish parks were established in the agricultural heartland, the anciently enclosed land that in Cornwall appears to have been farmed since at least the late first millennium BC (see Herring 1998). The three to six centuries of farming and field system development since disparking help explain why so few of the medieval parks located in this anciently enclosed land are clearly visible now.

Using the 1994 historic landscape characterisation (Cornwall County Council 1996) as a proxy for likely medieval land use, it is possible to establish that parks tended to have 20–30% of their area as steep-sided valleys containing woods, with relatively open or unwooded ground covering the remaining portion. There is some documentary support for this projected pattern. The Duchy park at Lanteglos in 1337 contained 102 acres of open, potentially arable land, making 83% of its area, 10 acres of meadow (8%), and 11 acres of wood pasture (9%) (Hull 1971, 24). In the far east, the Edgcumbes appear to have established two large parks in or around 1515, in two fairly different landscapes. That at their old home at Cotehele, in the middle Tamar, contained many steep slopes and had 160 acres of wood (32% of its extent), 100 acres of 'land', presumably arable (20%), 200 acres of pasture (40%), and 40 acres of furze and heath (8%). Mount Edgcumbe's park, at the Tamar's mouth and with gentler slopes, was more open, having just 60 acres of wood (12%), 300 acres of 'land' (58%), 50 acres of pasture (10%), and 100 acres of furze and heath (20%) (CRO, ME 682; notes taken by Cynthia Gaskell-Brown). Godolphin park had a mix of upland rough ground and anciently enclosed land and contained relatively little woodland, unless its north-west side reached down to the

River Hayle (see Herring 1997). Carn Brea was dominated by upland rough ground and included only a little woodland to its east, between the great hill and St Uny's church (see Tangye 1981, 34–5).

In thirteenth century Cornwall arable land was mainly in open fields, probably still largely unenclosed, although the progress of enclosure from that time (Herring 1986) meant that builders of later deer parks had to adapt to a landscape increasingly full of barriers. In the earlier period, however, lords had relative freedom to design their parks and some were created as nice ovals or rings in plan (as were many in England; Cantor 1982, 75). The perfect oval of Carn Brea's western part was planted on heathland but the roughly circular park at Lanteglos was imposed on farmland. By cutting through strip fields it usefully confirms an early date, pre-1271, for these strips. More parks were sub-rectangular or irregular in plan, their builders often working with the topography (including hedged lanes, existing patterns of fields, etc) rather than imposing a shape onto it.

As well as differences in shape, form of pale, and types of landscape enclosed, there was also considerable variety in scale. There were small parks of less than 50 acres beside castles at Launceston and Trematon; fourteenth-century records indicate that they were occasionally supplied with deer from Kerrybullock park. Other small parks, like Bennacott in Boyton (c.62 acres) or Pengersick in Breage (26.5 acres), may simply reflect the relatively modest wealth of their owners. They would not have been large enough for full-scale chases but would have served as stores of live deer, and other game animals like rabbits. At the other end of the range, Kerrybullock itself and Liskeard New Park and Restormel (465, 580, and 549 acres respectively when described post-disparkment in c.1640) were all large and each contained a substantial hunting lodge with several chambers (Pounds 1982, 78 and 111; 1984, 152). The later medieval deer parks at Cotehele and Mount Edgcumbe were also c.500 acres and that at Godolphin appears to have been c.400 acres at its maximum extent, again probably in the late medieval period (Herring 1997, 239).

Landscape Design (1)

Cornwall's dissected topography, with numerous deep valleys, allows us to identify deliberate use of natural land forms in medieval deer park design more easily than in less obviously topographically varied landscapes (like Cambridgeshire). Almost all Cornish medieval parks contained a deep wooded valley, and the visual impact achieved in positioning of the parkland in relation to that valley is of interest in terms of identifying landscape design. The undulating landscape gave the opportunity to position parks so that they were either on display (visible from outside and afar) or secluded (difficult to look into); we can find good examples of both.

Three early eastern parks, Restormel, Penhallam and Kenketh/Pinsla, share a particular landscape design which presumably reflects

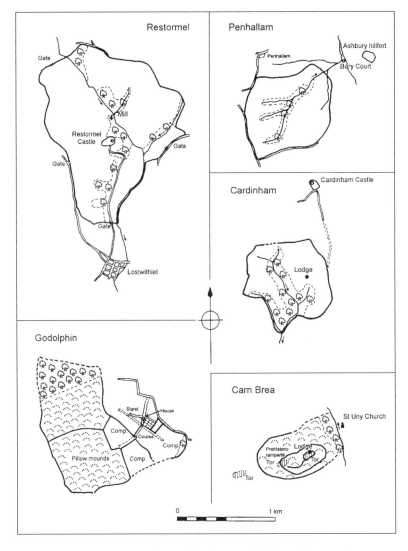

Fig. 18 Schematic plans of the three secluded Cardinan parks, Restormel, Penhallam and Cardinham (top), and the more openly displayed parks at Godolphin and Carn Brea (© Peter Herring)

their common origin, all being laid out by the powerful Cardinan family. All may have been created in the mid or late twelfth century (but presumably before Henry II imposed Forest Law on Cornwall). The earliest may be that at Kenketh/Pinsla, close to Cardinham castle, which could pre-date the family's marriage into the Bodardle family around 1166 that saw them move their power-base to the new town of Lostwithiel. Restormel park, immediately north of Lostwithiel, may have been laid out around 1166 as its interdependent relationship with the castle – probably of that period – suggests contemporaneity (see Thomas forthcoming for a discussion of Restormel and the lack of concrete evidence for a pre-Cardinan structure). The park was certainly extant by 1250 when the 'road to Restormel Park' was referred to in a document identifying a property in Lostwithiel (CRO, T445). Penhallam (Jacobstow) is adjacent to the family's thirteenth and fourteenth-century moated residence at Bury Court, the earliest stone structures at which have been dated to the late twelfth century (Beresford 1974). It is difficult to imagine Bury Court, remote from the family's main home at either Cardinham or Lostwithiel, being used other than occasionally and the proximity of a contemporary deer park (not identified by Beresford) provides a likely primary function for it as a hunting lodge (see Roberts 1988, 73 for equivalent 'houses' sited close to the Bishop of Winchester's parks).

Each of these Cardinan parks had the wooded valley centrally placed with more open land rising up on each side, but ending at or close to the ridgeline. They were not easily looked into from outside, and may have been considered quite private and secluded. The Cardinan estate was rather fragmented and in each case the family did not own much of the neighbouring land. The corollary effect gained when inside these parks was that from most points there was little sign of any other land, and especially land under the cultivation of peasants. An illusion was created that the park went on for ever, similar perhaps to a perfect dream forest, or a chase. It has perhaps been under-emphasised that parks, designed by lords, would have differed from forests and chases in this key way

– they did not contain the homes and fields of peasants, but were instead purely seigniorial, of and for the lord. The requirement in 1300 for all 13 villein tenants of Restormel manor to 'go to the lord's chace in the park once a year' (Hull 1971, xxxix) indicates that this was a regularly used hunting park in which the Earl and his guests pursued deer, presumably with dogs, for sport (see below), rather than simply a deer store. It may be suggested that the Earl's pleasure, and that of the hunting members of the great Cardinan family who created the parks, was enhanced by the cunningly contrived purity of the hunting landscapes in which they rode. At Restormel the riders would have seen the centrally positioned castle coming in and out of view as they moved around the dissected valley, and at Penhallam the moated site lay at the foot of the park, awaiting the hunters' triumphantly sweaty return.

The only important views outward from these three parks were at their lower ends and these were apparently carefully designed too. At Restormel, Lostwithiel town, largely controlled by the Cardinans, and after them, from 1268, by the Earls of Cornwall, closed off the lower end. At Kenketh/Pinsla a steep and probably wooded slope faced the lower part, continuing the dream park effect, and at Penhallam the valley was closed by a steep wooded hillside topped by a well-defined prehistoric hillfort (Ashbury), and with Bury Court at its foot.

In contrast to the seclusion of the Cardinan parks, the Basset family's fourteenth-century (or earlier) deer park on Carn Brea, the dominant hill of the Carnmenellis granite area, seems intended to have been seen and appreciated from a wide area, particularly from within that family's more consolidated estates. Peasant tenants may have leant on their shovels and gazed at their old hill to see the Bassets' pale encircling it, and seen deer, not sheep, moving across its face. People hunting or walking within the deer park, or sojourning at the summit 'castle' (perhaps more like another hunting lodge; Henderson 1935, 162), would have had extensive views over west Cornwall and to the sea. This park was, for Cornwall, unusually distant from the family home, Tehidy, but it appropriated for the Bassets' own use by far the most visually striking, prominent, and historically meaningful hill in the district. Additionally, in terms of identifying landscape design, only the two tors visible from Tehidy were enclosed by the pale; the third, western tor – not visible from Tehidy – was left unenclosed.

Godolphin deer park (dating uncertain, but possibly pre-sixteenth century) worked in a similar way to Carn Brea; appropriating a strik-ing and dominant hill, visible from much of west Cornwall, and enclosing it with a high pale, which itself cut across and made redund-ant the fields of medieval peasants (see Herring 1997).

The design of other medieval deer parks tended to fall between these extremes of con-tainment/privacy and openness/display. Earl-dom of Cornwall parks at Liskeard (Old) and

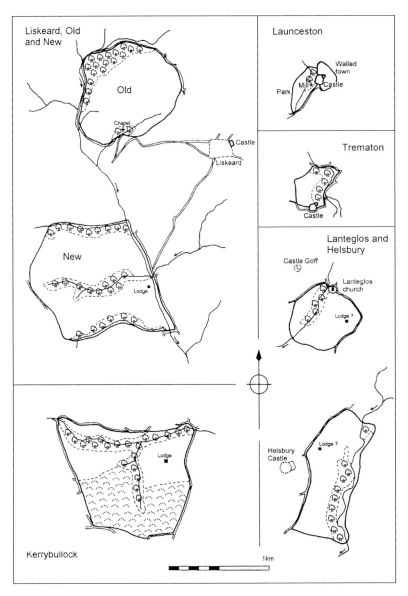

Fig. 19 Schematic plans of the other well-defined Earldom/Duchy of Cornwall parks; see Fig. 18 for Restormel (© Peter Herring)

Kerrybullock (both at least as early as the late thirteenth century) had main valleys to one side and parkland rising onto hills visible from afar and from which large extents of countryside could be seen.

Behaviour and Meaning

The historic landscape is a place filled with meaning. It is a text readable by those who lived in it or passed through it, and a canvas on which those with the power and will to do so could paint a socially or politically understandable representation of themselves. How then can we study deer parks to throw light on the people of medieval Cornwall? In particular what can they tell us about how members of the three estates – the lords, church and peasantry – might have perceived themselves?

Deer parks were expensive to build and maintain and probably involved overall financial loss to the lord who – while gaining some income from agistment, sale of timber etc – would also have given up revenue from the rent-producing farmland enclosed by the parks. See the Duchy of Cornwall's accounts (summarised in Hatcher 1970a) for details of fourteenth or fifteenth-century deficits. It may be supposed that lords in Cornwall had to pay for the construction of their parks, labour services being much less important here than in England (see Hatcher 1970b). They must also have been built at some cost – for example the pales themselves could only have been built at *c*.1–2m per person per day (judging from more recent rates for building stone walls; see Herring 1986). At such a rate the 7.2 kilometres long pale at Restormel would probably have taken at least 3,400 person days to build. In the 1340s, repairs to Restormel's pales (exceptionally made by tenants under obligation) were charged at one and a half pennies per day (Duchy Record Office, Minister's Accounts FD Vol. 7). Pale building alone may then have cost more than £20. The figure may have been much higher if costs associated with the Bishop of Winchester's park

at Bishop's Sutton (Hants.) can be used as a guide. Here *c*.2.4km of external pale and *c*.2km of internal banks appear to have taken around 6,000 days to build (i.e., less than 1m per day) and there were additional payments for carters and carpenters (Roberts 1988, 69–70). Other costs would have included the making of gates, building the walls or pales of any compartments, and the building of lodges; that at Helsbury cost at least £68 10s ½d in the mid fifteenth century (Hatcher 1970a).

Once constructed, the 'maintenance of the parks was a costly item of expenditure for the Duchy [of Cornwall]' (*ibid.*, 179). Full-time Duchy parkers were paid annual salaries ranging from 45s 6d to £4 11s and the pales required regular repair. Sometimes winter fodder had to be bought in for the deer. John Hatcher has calculated approximate annual running costs of the main Duchy parks in the fourteenth and fifteenth centuries at £7 to £8 for Restormel, £6 for Kerrybullock, £5 to £6 for Liskeard, and £4 for Helsbury, in total roughly 5% of the annual profits of the Duchy's Cornish manors (*ibid.*, 180, fig. 2).

To justify such costs, deer parks must have had significant meanings for their creators and served important functions. The Dukes of Cornwall very rarely used the Duchy parks; the Black Prince only visited Cornwall three times and hunted each time but there is no surviving documentation that any subsequent medieval Duke even came to the county (i.e. post-1376). As such, Hatcher felt that 'the parks constituted an expensive and rather unnecessary luxury' (Hatcher 1970a, 184) and that the de-parking by Henry VIII, albeit nearly two centuries after the Black Prince's time, 'was a sensible economy' (*ibid.*). In utilitarian terms this may indeed appear reasonable, but the fact that dozens of major and minor Cornish lords felt the need to spend considerable amounts of money on them indicates that parks clearly satisfied other less tangible but clearly important requirements.

We will discuss later how the creation of deer parks helped lords reinforce their political or feudal position through enclosure and exclusion: the imposition of their power on rural landscapes both real and social. First we should consider how deer (and other significant animals) contained within parks reflected and reinforced the lord's status.

The few medieval and early modern references to the animals themselves all indicate that Cornish parks held fallow deer. Two were stolen from Pawton park in 1301 (Henderson 1935, 159), four from Newham (near Truro) in 1304 (Pett 1998, 258), some from Penryn in 1330 (Henderson 1935, 159), and four from Lanteglos and Helsbury in 1364 (Henderson nd). Fawns, the young of the fallow deer, were recorded at Carrybullock, Liskeard, Restormel and Trematon parks in 1337 (Hull 1971, 42, 72, 116, and 122). The medieval deer bones excavated from Launceston Castle were also overwhelmingly of fallow deer, with very small numbers of roe and red deer (Albarella and Davis 1996, tables 1 and 5). Fallow deer were the favourite hunting animal, apparently deliberately introduced by the Normans to provide sport (Birrell 1992, 123).

Medieval deer management or farming was sophisticated and sensitive (*ibid.*, for a thorough review). It required access to a variety of habitats: meadows, open ground, and cover, as well as reliable water. Sometimes additional fodder had to be provided, as at Restormel where hay racks were installed (Hatcher 1970a, 180), and grasslands were occasionally improved, as in 1358 when the launds (grass-dominated compartments) at Restormel and Launceston were ploughed to renew grass 'destroyed by mos [moss] growing on the same' (*Registers of Edward the Black Prince*, Folio 86).

The male fallow deer, harts or bucks, were normally killed in the summer when they were carrying most meat and fat in preparation for the autumn rut (June to mid-September according to Birrell (1992, 122); Midsummer Day (June 24th) to the Festival of the Exaltation of the Holy Cross (September 14th) according to Trinick (1988, 246), the latter probably based on post-medieval prescriptions). Does or hinds, the female fallow deer were taken in the winter, late November to mid-February (Birrell 1992, 123) or Martinmas (11th November) to Candlemas (2nd February) according to Trinick (1988, 246). How the deer were dispatched is uncertain; medieval records are generally lacking. Some in the larger parks would have been taken by hunting, as in the annual 'chace' recorded at Restormel in 1300. As well as the thirteen villeins obliged to attend (Hull 1971, xxxix), the free conventionary tenants 'acted as huntsmen and grooms for the Duke, or anyone hunting in his name' at Restormel, and also at Lanteglos (*ibid.*, xxxiv–xxxv). We can look across southern England to the Bishop of Winchester's Marwell Park, similar in size to the large Duchy ones, to catch a glimpse of the personnel, horses and dogs involved. There, in 1246-7, the Bishop employed three knight huntsmen, seven squires, the Bishop's huntsman, 20 grooms, 23 greyhounds and 18 brachets or hunting dogs (Roberts 1988, 71). Greyhounds, in the charge of fewterers, hunted by sight, brachet hounds, in the charge of berners, by smell (*ibid.*, 72). It may be noted that John Lercedekne rendered the Duke one greyhound for the manor of Ellerkey (in Veryan) in 1337 (Hull 1971, 12).

There would have been no disruptive 'chace' on horseback in the 'fence month', around midsummer, when the hinds fawned and had to be left untroubled. There might, however, have been a 'stable', that is an organised shooting of selected deer from butts, the deer being driven (Roberts 1988, 72-3). A third form of sport was 'coursing', popular in the highest levels of society from the early sixteenth century. In this two or more greyhounds pursued a single deer along a measured course, spectators placing bets on the dogs and watching them cross a finishing line from a stand (e.g. Fretwell 1995). It is possible that all three methods were employed at Godolphin in the later medieval period: the main part of the park on Godolphin Hill was large enough for a chase; curious wide walls at the lower edges of the park, near the house, may have served both as walks and butts for 'stables'; and a course complete with a possible stand has been identified alongside the medieval gardens (Herring 1997; John Phibbs and John Schofield, pers. comm.).

Not all of the deer would have been killed during formal sporting events; most are likely to have been killed by estate workers either to order or culled to keep populations healthy. As is well known, the deer's flesh or venison was high status meat, eaten fresh or salted at feasts or presented as gifts to peers (Stamper 1988). At Launceston Castle in the medieval period, over 80% of the fallow deer venison appears to have been supplied as hind-limb haunches, apparently already detached from the pelvis, and possibly supplied from larger parks; the remaining small percentage may have been either hunted or shot in the adjacent small park (Albarella and Davis 1996, 32–4).

Rabbits and other small game were often raised within deer parks (Bond 1994, 116). Again Godolphin's park contains the best-preserved pillow mounds in Cornwall, eight rectangular and one circular. The high status

Fig. 20 Launceston from the south-west; see Fig. 21 for simplification (CAU F41/133, June 1993; © Cornwall County Council). Note the large window in the high tower overlooking the deer park in the lower left part of the picture

of the rabbit in the later medieval period was perhaps combined with its symbolic importance, representing both fecundity and religious Salvation (Stocker and Stocker 1996; Everson 1998) and is perhaps signified here by the prominent positioning of the two highest pillow mounds on the skyline of Godolphin Hill when viewed from the house and gardens (Herring 1997). Such a clear display of an overtly Catholic symbol might indicate a pre-Protestant

phase of the family's history for the dating of warren and deer park, adding weight to a suggested dating for the Godolphin park complex complementing the revised, earlier sixteenth century, dating of the King's Garden (Schofield 1999). It could be earlier than 1537, when Sir William Godolghan I suppressed a Catholic uprising in St Keverne (Herring 1997, 388).

Deer parks were not only home for the lord's fallow deer, and in some cases arenas for his

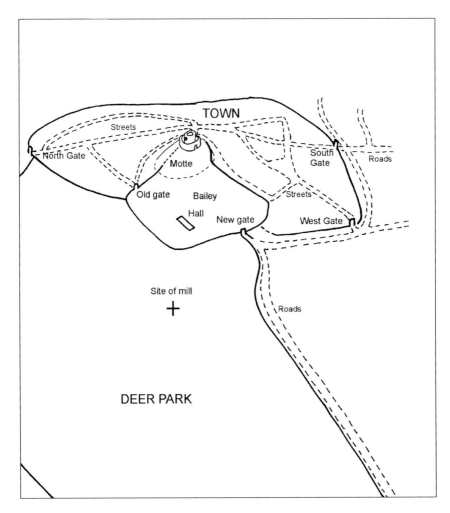

Fig. 21 Launceston, based on Fig. 20, showing the medieval castle and approaches to the southern entrance confined by the town wall and park pale. The Great Hall has been picked out in the bailey and the known medieval streets and likely medieval roads have also been indicated (© Peter Herring)

and his guests' sport; they were also attractive landscapes, capable of being appreciated by owners and guests. The blocks of woodland, wood pasture, open ground and meadows, indicated in documents and suggested by the variety of landforms enclosed, may have been arranged to enhance the relatively exotic, or at least less mundane or ordinary character of these places. We should note again the potential that parks gave lords to exclude the trappings of ordinary life – the cultivated land and the homes of ordinary people etc – that the earlier more open hunting grounds, the forests and chases, did not. A novel purity of design and experience could be achieved and enjoyed.

That deer parks also meant something to a lord's peers is indicated by the many instances of 'breaking' and deer-theft by other lords, a practice akin in some ways to early Irish (and perhaps also early Cornish) cattle-raiding. For example, Carn Brea park was broken in 1348 by John de Lambourn and Reginald de Bevyle (Tangye 1981, 34); these were not much like starving peasants poaching in desperation, but two of the Bassets' neighbouring landowners (with properties in Perranzabuloe and Gwinear) and their cocking a snook at Basset not only reveals interesting tensions between local lords (for more of which see Page 2000), but also the significance of parks and their deer as indicators of status and position in local society. There were also revealing clashes between rival men of the cloth. James de Kancia and Walter, the rector of Boconnoc – where the fine deer park may have already been in place – were accused in 1301 of breaking into the Bishop of Exeter's Pawton Park and taking two fallow deer. A Sir Thomas de Kancia, also of Boconnoc, had previously, in 1274, led an attack on the Bishop's park at Lanner (now Bishop's Wood), on behalf of the Earl of Cornwall (Henderson 1935, 159). A third park of the Bishop, at Penryn, was broken regularly in the early fourteenth century (1311, 1329, and 1330), and the Bishop strongly suspected that canons from the adjacent Glasney College were among the guilty, gaining access to the park and its fallow deer through their postern doors; he threatened miscreants with excommunication in 1330 (Peter 1903, 47–9).

In 1343, Duke Edward, the Black Prince, complained in a Commision of oyer and terminer, that the Duchy's rights had been violated by a long list of people including the Bishop of Exeter, Priors of St Michael's Mount, Bodmin, Launceston and Tywardreath, the Dean of St Buryan, four knights, forty-five other named people (a few from outside Cornwall), 'and others'. Violations included usurping the right to wreck and avoiding tax on tin. The accused had also, 'rescued distraints and attachments made by his ministers' and, most significantly for us, 'broke his parks at Liskeard, Kerrybullock, Restormel and Trematon, and hunted in these and carried away his deer' (Calendar of Patent Rolls, 1343, Feb 4). These activities may or may not have represented a concerted challenge to the Duchy's authority in the county (they are just as likely to have occurred piecemeal over the six years since the Duchy's creation, though see Page 2000 for further suggestions of tensions between the later medieval Cornish community and the Earldom and Duchy). The Prince's reaction, however, placing the parks' violation alongside significant losses to his income, confirms that the parks themselves and the deer within them were to some extent regarded as symbols of that authority.

It may be significant in terms of what deer parks, or their owners, meant to people that most of the late thirteenth and early fourteenth century 'park breaks' recorded in the Patent Rolls for which breakers' names are not recorded (and who may therefore have not been fellow lords but poorer people) were on parks of the Earldom and from 1337 the Duchy of Cornwall, both held of the Crown. If these were regarded as representing the nation, the unnamed breaks could be seen as signifying some sort of social or political protest.

We can begin then to understand what deer parks meant for the lord, or the bishop and priest. To reinforce associations with power, several deer parks apparently deliberately incorporated contemporary or past symbols of power: prehistoric forts within the parks at Carn Brea, Lanner, Swannacott, and Tremayne and contemporary parish churches on the boundary of Lanteglos and very near parks at

Carn Brea, Lesnewth and Launcells. As we have seen, the Bishop of Exeter also established a park against the walls of Glasney College.

We can also explore what deer parks might have meant for Cornish peasants. Peasants did not design the parks, though they would probably have been paid to build them. The deer parks were, however, imposed on the peasants' landscape, a landscape that though not owned by them had previously been open or accessible to them and, to varying extents, farmed and used by them.

It is not difficult to imagine the park being perceived by the Cornish peasant as symbolising three inter-related aspects of their social lives: powerlessness; lowliness of rank; and separation or exclusion.

Though some parks would have been established on demesne lands, many, especially the large ones, must have involved the dislocation of peasants' homes, the abandonment of hamlets, and the loss of fields, meadows and woodland. Liskeard (New) and Restormel, both in good farming country, probably displaced several hamlets, and at Lanteglos the park's curving boundary clearly cuts medieval strip fields, as does that at Godolphin (Herring 1997). Liskeard (Old) park appears to have enclosed and replaced a single township with a well-developed medieval strip based field system. Creation of the Arundell deer park at Lanhadron in St Ewe shortly after acquisition around 1433 involved the loss of the settlement and fields of 'Hallendaves' and half of 'Penbruglith' (see Fox and Padel 2000, 52). At Helsbury tenants had to accept exchanges of land when the park was extended before 1337 (Hatcher 1970a, 179) and there would have been losses in commons, or at least changes to rights, at heathy parks like Kerrybullock, Carn Brea and Godolphin. Cattle might still have been pastured with permission in these deer parks but the peasants' sheep were exchanged for the lord's deer, an animal without wool and whose flesh the peasant should not eat.

Peasant economies and family security must have been affected, presumably with little or no discussion; the lines of deer parks' boundaries appear to show no flexibility towards the peasant, cutting across fields and commons. The re-routing of roads closed by parks would have also affected the ordinary people of Cornwall. The Hundreds of Pydar and Powder accused the Bishop of Exeter of having blocked public highways at Pawton and Lanner before 1283, but he showed that he had provided alternative routes (Henderson 1935, 159). Diverted roads can be identified at most other Cornish deer parks; routes being abruptly deviated and run around their perimeters. Diversions would of course have caused inconvenience, but would also have emphasised the peasant's own impotence through the loss of customary rights and the disruption to familiar ways of moving about their world.

Park-related labour services were imposed on Duchy tenants. We have seen the Restormel villein tenants attending 'the lord's chace' and other tenants repairing pales. In a county where labour services were unusual it may have been considered particularly meaningful to have had to serve the lord in his park.

Medieval peasants would have known their rank already, of course. The local deer park vividly reminded the Cornish peasant of who he or she was. It also added to the peasant's awareness of social structure a sense of exclusion and separation. As we have seen, deer parks were designed not only for keeping deer in, but also for keeping people out. This was particularly meaningful when the park enclosed land that had previously been open or accessible.

Social separation was a developing trend visible elsewhere in medieval society. In the castles where the lord had previously mixed with all and sundry there was from at least the later thirteenth century increasing separation of the lord's family and guests from the rest of the household, and from each other (Girouard 1980). The churches, previously open public spaces, were also changing; the priest, after the acceptance of transubstantiation, dealt with Christ's body and blood in the increasingly screened-off chancel area (Holdsworth 1991, 29–30). The contemporary notion of purgatory and the increasingly sophisticated burial practices intended to guide people successfully through it reinforced a developing awareness of the importance of the individual as opposed to the communal (e.g. Gittings 1988). The deer park may be regarded as the landscape equivalent of this process; the fragmentation, enclosure and appropriation of previously open and accessible countryside. It could also be seen as containing and making more pure a sport that had previously ranged through much less restrictive forests and chases.

In many parts of Cornwall the deer park would have been the first example of restricted outdoor space, of explicitly private property. Elements of deer parks' design emphasised this separation. By running newly diverted roads or paths around the park's perimeter, the lord not only gave travellers the shortest alternative route, though usually annoyingly less convenient than before, but also presented them with a close view of the reason for their detour; to their side would have been the pale of the park of a powerful person. In a culture of increasing separation and closer definition of personal position, this was simple and effective landscape design.

The deer park therefore represented in the landscape the gradual increase in the separation of society's parts. It made manifest an aspect of contemporary ideology, the basis of our own individualised and hierarchical society, more visibly and powerfully than almost any other artificial creation. Landscape signals like deer parks might have helped such an ideology trickle down the social scale. It is in the thirteenth century, shortly after the earliest Cornish parks, that we get the earliest clear examples of social separation at the peasant level of Cornish society: the creation of private inner rooms in longhouses and the enclosure of field systems and the farming of individual holdings, separate from the rest of the community (Herring 1986).

Landscape Design (2)

More sophisticated examples of designed landscapes associated with castles and parks can be identified in medieval Cornwall. Paul Everson has suggested regarding castles that 'we should anticipate there will have been a carefully manipulated landscape whenever we look at the sites and setting of these great medieval buildings' (Everson and Brown 2000, 115). He illustrated this elegantly at Ludgershall in Wiltshire. Here the northern of two deer parks, together with the town and roads were intimately related to the late twelfth century stone castle, 'providing not just the setting but actually the substance of the castle . . . [which] was sited with care for effect and allusion' (*ibid.*).

At Launceston roadways guided travellers into Richard, Earl of Cornwall's controlled and dramatic later medieval landscape, a landscape in which the deer park played a part. The great Norman castle looked east and west respectively on a walled town (early thirteenth century) and the deer park (earliest reference 1282, but possibly contemporary with the town walls). These confined and funnelled the only external approach to the castle's new and barbicanned southern gate (see Saunders 1977), possibly built as one with the town wall and the park. Unless they had passed through the gates and streets of the town to reach the bailey's earlier but now lesser northern entrance, people riding or walking up to the impressive new gate would have been funnelled by the town wall and park pale. Along this road they were obliged to view an impressive arrangement of symbols and proofs of the power and wealth of the Earls and Dukes of Cornwall. Principally, the great shell keep with its new high tower set at the rear of a busy bailey and framed by a walled town and a paled park. Rob Liddiard (2000) has illustrated a very carefully controlled approach to Castle Rising in north Norfolk which involved visitors being guided past several symbols of the owner's power (including a planned town) before arriving at the castle. This had a deer park wrapped around its rear, on higher ground, providing approaching travellers with a dramatic backdrop to the castle but also preventing approaches from that quarter.

Once inside the bailey at Launceston, the motte and the castle's walls against the town blocked views north, east and south. Although secondary to the Norman bailey, the park and its deer were carefully positioned to dominate the foreground of the longest, westward views, left open by building the bailey's west wall along the base of the gently sloping ground above the steeper valley slopes below. The broad terrace walk carefully created on the north-eastern rampart of Ludgershall Castle, apparently contemporary with the late twelfth-century Great Tower and associated royal lodgings, allowed a view of the deer park to the north (Everson and Brown 2000, 101). Princess Isabella's balcony at Woodstock Palace in Oxfordshire was apparently built to obtain a similar view over Woodstock Park (Stamper 1988, 143). The only substantial first floor window in Earl Richard's mid thirteenth-century high tower, on top of Launceston's motte, gives awkward, craning, downward views onto the bailey's north gate but much more comfortable ones, from carefully constructed window seats, across the bailey and valley to the deer park.

Within Launceston's park was the Castle or Park Mill; those bringing grain or collecting flour would presumably have entered the park along prescribed routes. Arwenack park contained a windmill and there was also a mill in Restormel park (probably to the north-east of the castle where a 'Mill Moor' was recorded in 1840; Lanlivery Tithe Apportionment, Field Number 1086). Several Earldom and Duchy bureaucratic functions were also performed at Restormel Castle, obliging people to regularly pass through the park to visit it on business. In 1312, for example, all tin-workers and others with tin for sale were ordered to 'cause their tin to be carried to the king's castle of Rustelmer' [Restormel] (Cal of Close Rolls, Oct 8, 1312). Restormel park had at least three gates, but most people probably entered through 'Towney Gate' at the lower, Lostwithiel end. As noted earlier, views here were carefully designed to display little but deer park, and those from the 'Towney Gate' road, beside the Fowey River, were particularly restricted. Travellers making for the castle rising up ahead of them would have seen only deer park, private land. Local people would have known that this was previously open country, land they once had access to.

Other later medieval parks similarly containing their owners' castles or principal houses were at Bodrugan, Arwennack, Cotehele (main park), and possibly Bicton (St Ive) and we may expect approaches at some or all of these to have also been carefully manipulated.

At Godolphin, at the very end of the medieval period, the deer park was fully integrated into a complex designed landscape, much of which survives in remarkably good condition. The eastern approach to the house passed alongside the park's pale and the great house and its compartmentalised terraced gardens were linked to the park via a series of raised walks. One ran around the garden giving views both inward to knotworks, ponds, etc, and also out to grazing deer or coursing hounds. Other raised walks led up towards the hill where horse riders would have chased the deer, horns blowing, hounds baying. At other times, driven deer could have been shot from these same walks (Herring 1997; Schofield 1999).

Medieval deer parks were, then, designed landscapes in which there was participation, movement, and occasional noise; landscapes that were experienced as much as contemplated. This active element may be the main difference between medieval deer parks and the more serene landscape parks of the early modern period, more peacefully studied from particular viewpoints.

Deer parks can be viewed then as more than just status symbols. They were dynamic creations, reflecting changes in society and possibly helping to stimulate further change.

Much more work could be done on Cornish parks. As well as searching for unrecorded sites (for example on the knightly and church estates), some known parks require precise location and many more need to have their extent and content established. Once this is done they can be assessed to establish how they were designed. All medieval castles and moated or enclosed country houses could be reviewed to determine functional and aesthetic relationships with any associated parks (and gardens). More documentary work could be done on Earldom and Duchy of Cornwall parks, especially on modes of hunting and management of the deer. The Christian symbolism of deer could also be usefully pursued.

Acknowledgements

Without Rob Wilson-North's initial invitation to discuss Cornish deer parks, I would not have had the pleasure of reading Paul Everson, Twigs Way and Edward Roberts, the most substantial influences on this paper, nor of delving into an aspect of medieval Cornwall that had long seemed intriguing, but not pressingly so. Cathy Parkes and Graeme Kirkham refused to believe half of what I thought about parks and so improved all my arguments; Graeme, in Swindon, also provided me with literature difficult to obtain in Lostwithiel. John Schofield, Johnny Phibbs, Nigel Thomas, Pete Rose, Colin Buck, Ann Reynolds, Cynthia Gaskell-Brown, Sue Pring and Lewis Eynon all wittingly or unwittingly provided either information or ideas.

Abbreviations

CAU	Cornwall Archaeological Unit
CRO	Cornwall Record Office
RCHME	Royal Commission on the Historical Monuments of England

References

Albarella, U. and Davis, S.J.M. 1996 'Mammals and birds from Launceston Castle, Cornwall: decline in status and the rise of agriculture', *Circaea, Jnl of Assoc. for Environmental Archaeology* 12(1), 1–156

Beresford, G. 1974 'The Medieval Manor of Penhallam, Jacobstow, Cornwall' *Medieval Archaeol.* 18, 90–145

Birrell, J. 1992 'Deer and Deer Farming in Medieval England' *Agricultural History Review* 40(2), 112–126

Bond, J. 1994 'Forests, Chases, Warrens and Parks in Medieval Wessex', in M. Aston and C. Lewis (eds) *The Medieval Landscape of Wessex*

Borlase, Rev. W.1758 *The Natural History of Cornwall*

Brown, G. 1998 'Parklands as guardians of early landscapes: Highclere Castle, Hampshire' in P. Pattison (ed.) *There by Design*, RCHME and British Archaeological Reports, British Series 267, 7–12

Cantor, L. 1982 'Forests, chases, parks and warrens' In L. Cantor (ed.) *The English Medieval Landscape*, 56–85

Cantor, L.1983 *The Medieval Parks of England, a Gazetteer*

Carew, R. 1969 *The Survey of Cornwall* (first published 1602). Republished, edited and with an introduction, by Halliday, F.E., Kelley: New York.

Cornwall County Council, 1996 *Cornwall Landscape Assessment 1994*, text prepared by Landscape Design Associates and Cornwall Archaeological Unit, Truro

Everson, P. 1998 'Delightfully surrounded with woods and ponds: field evidence for medieval gardens in England' in P. Pattison (ed.) *There by Design*, RCHME, British Archaeological Reports, British Series 267, 32–8

Everson, P. and Brown, G. 2000 'The earthworks, and landscape context' in Everson, P., Brown, G. and Stocker, D., 'The castle earthworks and landscape context', in Ellis, P. (ed.) *Ludgershall Castle, Excavations by Peter Addyman 1964–1972, Wilts Archaeol. and Nat. Hist. Soc., Monograph No 2*, 97–115

Everson, P. and Williamson, T. 1998 'Gardens and designed landscapes', in P. Everson and T. Williamson (eds) *The Archaeology of Landscape*

Fox, H.S.A. and Padel, O.J. 2000 *The Cornish Lands of the Arundells of Lanherne, 14th to 16th centuries*, Devon and Cornwall Record Society, NS 41

Fretwell, K. 1995 'Lodge Park, Gloucestershire; a rare surviving deer course and Bridgeman layout' *Garden History* 23.2, 133–44

Gilbert, C.S. 1817 and 1820 *Historical Survey of Cornwall, Vols 1 and 2*,

Girouard, M. 1980 *Life in the English Country House, a social and architectural history*

Gittings, C. 1988 *Death, burial and the individual in early modern England*

Hatcher, J. 1970a *Rural Economy and Society in the Duchy of Cornwall 1300–1500*

Hatcher, J. 1970b 'Non-Manorialism in Medieval Cornwall', *Agr. Hist. Rev.* 18, 1–16

Henderson, C. (nd) 'Deer parks' unpub. mss held at the Courtney Library, Royal Cornwall Museum

Henderson, C. 1935 *Essays in Cornish History*

Herring, P.C. 1986 *An Exercise in Landscape History, Pre-Norman and Medieval Brown Willy and Bodmin Moor*, Unpub. MPhil thesis, University of Sheffield.

Herring, P.C. 1997 *Godolphin, Breage, an archaeological and historical assessment*, Cornwall Archaeological Unit, Truro

Herring, P.C. 1998 *Cornwall's Historic Landscape, presenting a method of historic landscape assessment*, Cornwall Archaeological Unit, Truro

Herring, P.C., Thorpe, C. and Morley, B. 1998 *Pengersick, Breage, an archaeological and historical assessment*, Cornwall Archaeological Unit, Truro

Hitchins, F. and Drew, S. 1824 *The History of Cornwall*, 2 volumes, Helston

Holdsworth, C. 1991 'From 1050 to 1307' in N. Orme (ed.) *Unity and Variety, a history of the Church in Devon and Cornwall*, 23–52

Hoppit, R. 2000 'Suffolk parks and the process and pattern of settlement', talk given to Medieval Settlement Research Group, University of East Anglia

Hull, P.L. (ed.) 1971 'The Caption of Seisin of the Duchy of Cornwall' *Devon and Cornwall Record Society NS 17*

Liddiard, R. 2000 Castle Rising, 'A Landscape of Lordship', talk given to Medieval Settlement Research Group, University of East Anglia

Lysons, D. and Lysons, S. 1814, *Magna Britanniae, volume the third, Cornwall*

Norden, J. 1966 *Speculi Britanniae Pars. A Topographical and Historical description of Cornwall.* First published 1728, reprinted 1966

Padel, O.J. 1985 *Cornish Place-name Elements*, English Place-names Society LVI/LVII

Pattison, P. (ed.) 1998 *There by Design, Field Archaeology in Parks and Gardens*, RCHME and British Archaeological Reports, British Series 267

Peter, T.C., 1903 *The history of Glasney Collegiate Church, Cornwall*

Pett, D.E. 1998 *The Parks and Gardens of Cornwall*

Platt, C. 1978 *Medieval England*

Pounds, N.J.G. 1982 *The Parliamentary Survey of the Duchy of Cornwall, Pt 1, Devon and Cornwall Record Society, NS 25*

Pounds, N.J.G. 1984 *The Parliamentary Survey of the Duchy of Cornwall, Pt 2, Devon and Cornwall Record Society, NS 27*

Registers of Edward the Black Prince, 1348–1365, 4 vols (1930–3)

Roberts, E. 1988 'The Bishop of Winchester's Deer Parks in Hampshire, 1200–1400' *Proc. Hampshire Field Club Archaeol. Soc.*, 44, 67–86

Saunders, A. 1977 'Excavations at Launceston Castle 1970–76: Interim report' *Cornish Archaeol.*, 16, 129–37

Schofield, J. 1999 *Godolphin, The Garden evidence to date*

Shirley, E.P. 1867 *Some Account of English Deer Parks*

Stamper, P. 1988 'Woods and Parks' in G. Astill and A. Grant (eds.) *The Countryside of Medieval England*, 128–48

Tangye, M. 1981 *Carn Brea, brief history and guide*

Thomas, N. 1998 *Lanhydrock Park, a survey of an historic landscape*, Cornwall Archaeological Unit, Truro

Thomas, N. (forthcoming) 'Restormel Castle: A reappraisal' *Medieval Archaeol.*

Tonkin, T. (nd) *Parochial History of Cornwall*

Trinick, M. 1988 'The Deer Parks at Lanhydrock and Pinsla' *Jnl Royal Institution of Cornwall*, X(2), 221–52

Way, T. 1997 *A study of the impact of imparkment on the social landscape of Cambridgeshire and Huntingdonshire from c.1080 to 1760*, British Archaeological Reports, British Series, 258, Oxford

Postscript

The author is preparing a descriptive table of Cornish deer parks with a view to eventual publication; he would be happy to provide copies and would welcome comment and any additional information.

Dartington Hall & Shilston Barton: Archaeological Excavation at two Devon Gardens, 1991–2000

Christopher Currie

The author was invited by Michelle Marr (formerly Gregory) to present summaries of his recent work on two Devon gardens for this volume. These works have produced results of possible national importance. They were carried out as a training excavation at Dartington Hall between 1991 and 1999, and as an evaluation of an unusual building of possible garden design at Shilston Barton, Modbury, in the summer of 2000. The results given below are provisional views. It is hoped to publish the full results of both sets of work at a later date.

Dartington Hall: The Origins of the Gardens

Introduction

There has been a long-standing local tradition at Dartington that the terraced garden to the south of the hall was a medieval tiltyard.

Although the academic world has largely dismissed this claim (Emery 1975, 151–2), the story still has a strong hold on local people. Excavations in the gardens between 1991 and 1999 recovered good evidence to further demolish the 'tiltyard' tradition. This short essay looks at the history of the garden, as revealed by the most recent documentary researches and by archaeology, and discusses the true origins of the gardens.

Dartington Hall stands on high ground above the River Dart, to the north of Totnes, in the County of Devon (NGR SX 798 628). The Hall has been described by Pevsner as the 'most spectacular medieval mansion of Devon' (1952, 99). Its origins date back to Domesday and beyond. Its early history is obscure until the late fourteenth century when it became the principal seat of John Holand, half-brother to Richard II. He was largely responsible for converting the earlier manor house into a late medieval mansion more suited to a member of the royal family. In 1559 it was obtained by Sir Arthur Champernowne (DRO 215/1/3), and it remained with his family until 1925. The estate declined as a result of the agricultural depression of the later nineteenth century and the Hall was much neglected when purchased by the Elmhirsts in 1925. It was under Dorothy Elmhirst's direction that the gardens were laid out in their present form.

The Tiltyard Myth

The idea of the tiltyard may have originated in the minds of the Elmhirsts shortly after they purchased the Hall. An early photograph has a note attached by Leonard Elmhirst, which says 'Terraces probably untouched since fourteenth century. Mr Lynch [the head gardener] "did them up".' (Snell 1989, 26). Initially the area below the terraces was turned into an open-air theatre, with a raised stage at the east end. The conversion to the Tiltyard's present form was carried out in 1954–55. By this time Dorothy Elmhirst was certain of it having been a Tiltyard when she wrote that it would be '. . . turned back to its historic fourteenth century form as a tiltyard, flattening out the whole space to the level of the present stage with a flight of steps at the top.' (Snell 1989, 62).

The tradition that the area was a tiltyard may not pre-date the Elmhirsts' arrival at Dartington in 1925. When Christopher Hussey wrote his *Country Life* article on the hall in 1938, he said of the terraces:

> *It has been suggested by Mr. Elmhirst, in explanation of this remarkable arrangement – and I feel in agreement with him – that the amphitheatre was formed out of a natural dell to provide a tiltyard, and that the arcade [the ruined arches on the south side of the private lawn] is the remains of a kind of "grand stand" incorporated in the outer side of the garden court.*
>
> (Hussey 1938, 208)

The Elmhirsts had learnt by this time that a former owner of the Hall, John Holand, Duke of Exeter and half-brother to Richard II (1377–99), was reputed to be a keen jouster. From this association, the terraces came to be seen as of fourteenth century date, as were the ruined arches on the south side of the private lawn.

This idea was initially taken up by Anthony Emery who went on to quote dimensions for the ideal tournament ground, 60 by 40 yards, as defined by a medieval duke of Gloucester, as corresponding with the area of the lawn at the bottom of the terraces (Emery 1958, 201–2). This area is not 60 yards by 40, but an irregular shape that only attains a width of 40 yards at one point. This was excused on the argument that the dimensions were not exact because of the natural form of the dell in which it was built (*ibid.*, 202).

In 1962 Colin Platt was asked to do an archaeological excavation on the private lawn to confirm the conjectured date for the building of which the ruined arches had once formed a part. The idea behind this was that as this building was clearly at a strange angle to the fourteenth century Hall, but was parallel with the terraces, the symmetry was a result of the arches and the Tiltyard being contemporary. It was therefore expected that Platt would confirm the fourteenth century date to establish John Holand as the builder of the terraces (Platt 1962, 208).

Despite a heavy bias on the expected final outcome of the excavations, Platt argued that the arches dated from *c*.1500. He concluded therefore that there was 'no positive evidence whatever for the dating of the so-called tournament ground . . .' and that 'any argument for an early dating of the south courtyard that depended on the alignment of the buildings with the tournament ground and on John Holand's acknowledged prowess as a jouster would be unsatisfactory' (*ibid.*, 219).

Although Anthony Emery had some difficulty with some of Platt's results, he later came round to the view that the terraces were not made as a tiltyard. In a 1975 essay he concluded that tournament grounds were not laid out in such confined spaces, but were more like cricket pitches (Emery 1975, 151–3). He discussed the subject at some length concluding: '. . . further research and the excavation of the south court has convinced me that the terraces are a post-medieval feature and that they bear no relation to the construction of the gallery or the south court' (*ibid.*, 151).

In spite of this conclusive dismissal of the old

arguments, the tradition continued. As late as 1989, Reginald Snell appears to disregard Platt's evidence when he says of the Tiltyard: '. . . there is very good historical evidence that it was used as such [as a tiltyard] in the early part of the fifteenth century.' (Snell 1989, 16).

The persistence of the myth in Snell's opinion is even more remarkable in that, in his book on the gardens, *From the bare stem* (1989) he makes it quite clear that he is aware that the 'Tiltyard' floor had once contained a formal garden, known as the Dutch Garden, and that the levels were much higher before the Elmhirsts' purchase of the Hall. In this book, he presents evidence that shows that the 'Tiltyard' does not appear to be known by that name until given it by the Elmhirsts on no evidence other than their personal opinion, or local hearsay.

The Terraces as a Formal Garden

The Elmhirsts were clearly aware that the level below the terraces was once much higher than the present floor. They were also aware that the area was known as the Dutch Garden, and had been in that form since at least the 1850s.

The earliest accurately dated evidence for this garden is the 25" Ordnance Survey map of 1889 (WCSL sheet 121.1). This shows a formal *parterre* at the level of the Irish yews known as the Twelve Apostles. An undated photograph (DH Garden/1) in the Hall confirms this. On the reverse, written presumably by one of the Elmhirsts, are notes, which date the picture to *c.*1864. This is remarkably early for an outdoor photograph, but not impossible. The yews are shown much smaller, and seem to have been planted about 20–25 years before the picture was taken. The notes state that the revetment wall to the Bowling Green was raised in the first years of the Elmhirsts' residence to prevent children falling over it. Another photograph, hanging in the bar of the White Hart (DH Garden/2), shows the Dutch Garden at an apparently later date. This is reproduced in Snell's book, but without a caption. The much greater size of the yews indicates the later date.

An Ordnance Survey map of 1904 (WCSL,

sheet 121.1) shows the valley floor still at the same level as the yews, but no longer shows the *parterre*. Although this leads one to suppose it had been abandoned by this date, this does not seem to have been the case. Snell describes the area when the Elmhirsts first arrived:

> At one point an old cider press was discovered in the undergrowth, and moved to the centre of a square lawn in the Dutch garden that the earlier Champernownes had made at the upper end of the Tiltyard. At its lower end there had evidently once been a formal rose garden, only slightly below the level of the Twelve Apostles, but this had been filled in, and was now . . . little more than a large and unsightly hole. (Snell 1989, 22)

Snell further records that the terraces were much degenerated when the Elmhirsts first arrived, and are described from a contemporary photograph as being merely 'gently undulating slopes'. They appear to have been drastically restored by Stewart Lynch after 1928 (*ibid.*, 26), and so it is difficult to be sure how close they come to their original profile on the south side. On the north side of the Tiltyard their shape seems to correspond well with those of the present.

Records in the Devon Record Office help to unravel the mystery of the garden terraces. These include some of the Champernowne's records, miscellaneous eighteenth century sketches and other pictures, a volume of proposals for alterations to the Hall in 1805 by George Sanders, plus a family history of the Champernownes written in 1954 by Miss C. E. Champernowne (Emery 1958, *passim*).

There are also some valuable clues surviving in the archives still at Dartington. As well as transcripts made of some of the Champernowne's deeds, there is a fine collection of drawings, paintings, prints and early photographs available. These include a watercolour by Archdeacon Froude of *c.*1801 showing the south side of the Hall (DH Froude). This seems to show a substantial wall, with a possible buttress, or projecting building, in the foreground that can not be related to any surviving building. The picture is badly faded, and is not clear on detail or perspective, making interpretation difficult.

A copy of the 1839 Tithe Map survives in the Dartington archive (DH tithe). This shows a square building on the lawn in front of what are now the private apartments, but not the wall shown by Froude. The tithe map also fails to show the terraces in the garden. This has caused all sorts of interpretative problems. It might be argued that they existed, but that the tithe map did not show them because they were not relevant to the map's purpose. This might be the case, but it is curious that hundreds of other tithe maps across the country frequently show garden designs with great accuracy. The other answer is that the terraces simply did not exist at this time.

This has caused garden historians a further problem. The terraces are very much in the style one might expect of later seventeenth and early eighteenth century formal gardens. A line of sweet chestnuts stand on the upper terrace that are reputed to be 300 years, a date their appearance does not contradict. However, these may mark an early boundary that the garden chose to respect. They do not necessarily argue that the garden could not have been laid out inside their line at any time after their planting.

A recent examination of documents in the Devon Record Office may help to clarify the date of the garden, and produce a reasonable hypothesis on when and why the terraces were created. The most interesting records are a series of drawings and plans made to coincide with proposed alterations to the hall in the first half of the nineteenth century.

These proposals came about through the desire of one of the many of Arthur Champernowne's desire to rebuild the hall into a more substantial mansion more suited to its, even then, great fame as a medieval building. This Arthur owned Dartington from 1774 until 1819, but it was not until 1805 that he conceived of his plan to turn his home into a great example of the then fashionable Gothic Revival style. It is perhaps ironic that there was once an elaborate south court that had been subsequently demolished. A ground plan of the hall produced at that time shows the Best Lawn surrounded by a wall. This includes the arches on its south side, clearly shown as such on the plan. It also shows Froude's wall, with what appears to be a summerhouse or similar building attached to the outside. This wall had been destroyed by the time of the tithe map of 1839, but the attached building remained, itself disappearing by the time of the earliest large-scale OS map of 1889.

A damaged plan of 1805 shows Dartington and its immediate environs before the proposed alterations were put forward. This does not show the terraces, just a single terrace below the arches, with a square pond in the valley below (DRO Z15/38/1/7/1). It has always been the contention of Graham Gammin, the present gardens manager, that the Tiltyard valley was the prefect place to build a pond, and here, it appears we have evidence to support his feeling. It is curious that the writer of the unpublished Champernowne history knew of this plan, but was apt to dismiss that the pond could have existed on the most illogical of reasons that it had 'a stream running through it' (Champernowne 1954, 283). Most historic ponds were created in valleys with streams running through them (*cf.* Currie 1988 *passim*).

If this plan is accepted, and there is no good reason why it should not be, then the absence of terraces on the tithe map becomes instantly explainable. Other references from the Champernowne archive support the view that there were no terraces before 1839. A release and quitclaim of Edward Champernowne to Arthur Champernowne dated February 1682 describes the hall and its gardens:

All title to the manors of Dartington . . . and in particular to the Newhouse on the north side of the garden called the fine garden, the three inner chambers, the higher larder, the higher dairy, the garner chamber over the gatehouse, the toolhouse under it, the hay tallet over the higher stable . . . 2 cellars at the lower end of the great hall, the drilling house, the higher barn, the stable adjoining, the Barne orchard, the Rookehay orchard alias the Rickhay orchard, Alley park . . . the 2 Symons Trees, on the east of the way from Dart house to the parson-

age house . . . the Churchyard close or meadow, and the Little Close and the moiety of the fine garden, the kitchen garden and the shippen.

(DRO Z15/1/22/2)

The 'Newhouse' appear to refer to that section of the complex known as the Upper Residential Wing (often incorrectly called the Georgian Wing). The 'fine garden' would therefore be the Best Lawn. If this is correct it would suggest that previous interpretations of Dartington are incorrect. The wing, which became the main residential block of the Champernownes was not built in the 'Georgian' period, as previously thought, but seems to have been a fairly new creation in 1682. If the 'fine garden' existed then it suggests that the south court was demolished at some time before 1682. The field names given relate to the land units around the hall and church, many of which survive on the tithe survey, and it should be noted that there is no reference to the terraces being part of any garden. It might be reasonable to conclude that they did not exist at this date.

During the drawing up of the proposals of 1805, a number of descriptions of the surrounding land are given. A caption to one of the proposal plans states:

The gallery and terrace before it [the Bowling Green] are situated where there appears to have been a gallery and terrace in the original building, commanding the best prospects and looking over a steep declivity which together with the hanging woods at the north west end of the terrace, admit of being rendered an agreeable spot. The hanging woods may be approached by a walk united to that end of the terrace'.

(DRO Z15/38/1/7/10)

The plan is then produced as a painting of the proposal. The caption here states:

The high mounds, and woods upon them, which surround the present buildings, prevented a correct view being taken of the grounds: this is therefore done [the painting] from recollection of the relative situation of the parts and as they may

be disposed. The lawn [possibly a grassy area in the valley floor adjoining the pond], here represented at some depth below the front of the terrace [the Bowling Green], is at present, flat, the substratum of which is stone that may be cut away and employed in raising the terrace . . . This view has been given to shew the . . . principal front . . . but the grandest and that which this design has principally had to respect, will be from the usual walk ascending to Dartington Hall from Totnes and the river, which will present the tower at the angle and the high terrace, overlooking a considerable declivity, and that view will produce the true castellated appearance.

(DRO Z15/38/1/12)

In all this talk of what a steep slope there was from the Bowling Green to the valley floor, there is not one mention of terraces. Others have noted that of all the antiquarian descriptions of Dartington before 1839, there is not one mention of the terraces in the valley (Emery 1975, 151–2). Instead there are these other descriptions, which although not entirely clear, suggest a completely different layout.

Arthur Champernowne did not carry out his grand scheme. He went as far as to take the roof off the Great Hall to examine the timbers, and found their replacement so expensive that he decided to leave it off. He justified this by stating that 'when the walls of the hall are overgrown with ivy, they will be as admired as they are now' (Emery 1970, 88).

About 1845 the scheme to rebuild Dartington as a Gothic fantasy mansion was revived by Henry Champernowne. He got no less than the renowned Augustus Pugin, one of the leading proponents of the Gothic Revival, to draw up a new scheme to create another courtyard partly over the site of the south court. Plans were drawn up (DRO Z15/38/1/7/19–21), but, again, the scheme never came about. Some changes were made to the Solar block, which became the lower residential wing (Emery 1970, 88), but the revived south court remained unbuilt.

It is curious that our first evidence for the existence of the terraces, with the Dutch Garden in the floor of the valley, occurs not long after this episode. Henry Champernowne was attributed as having done much to improve the gardens, although the terraces are not specifically mentioned. It is not impossible that they are older than his time, but it is curious they are not mentioned. From the 1860s a series of illustrations and plans begin to show them fully formed. On balance of evidence, it would seem, therefore, that the terraces may have been created during Pugin's involvement at Dartington. As the scheme involved the revival of ancient forms of architecture, it was entirely in keeping that the gardens should be remodelled to compliment this air of antiquity that both Arthur and Henry Champernowne sought to create at Dartington.

Archaeological Excavations at Dartington, 1962 and 1991–9

Colin Platt found little evidence for fourteenth and fifteenth-century occupation in the area of the south court, although a possible earlier thirteenth-century building was uncovered. He considered that the buildings that were once sited on the private lawn dated to *c.*1500 (Platt 1962, 219). His conclusion that the buildings on the lawn were pulled down in the later seventeenth century coincides with the reference to the 'fine garden' existing in 1682 given above. The area may then have been levelled for a formal garden. Later, probably in the early nineteenth century, more levelling occurred to make the present lawned area (*op. cit.*, 219).

The excavations in the 1990s by this author largely complimented Platt's work on the Best Lawn. A complete plan was recovered for the squarish building that Platt called the 'tower', and further parts of the west end of the adjoining south range were excavated. Like Platt, it was discovered that the build up of terrace was of some depth, being over 1.5m deep in places. Consequently it was rare for the excavations to get down to the original ground surface.

The more recent work found Platt's plan of the site to be a simplification of what was actually there. At least three phases were recognised in the buildings of the South Court. These were overlain by Archdeacon Froude's garden wall,

Fig. 22 Dartington Hall. The Best Lawn under excavation in 1993, with the terraces of the 'Tiltyard' in the background (© Christopher Currie)

a much cruder structure, dating to the late seventeenth or early eighteenth century on archaeological evidence. It was not possible to give exact dates for the three phases of the south court because the original ground surface was not reached. Architectural fragments, some of good quality, revealed that high status buildings had existed here dating from the later fifteenth or early sixteenth century. A large fragment of a flat-headed Perpendicular window was recovered from the rubble. Finds were numerous, particularly pottery, but this dated mainly from the sixteenth and seventeenth centuries, again supporting Platt's view that there was much activity in the area at that time.

Although the evidence was far from clear, it seems that of the three phases, one was clearly dated to around 1500. Unfortunately it is not possible to say which one, but it would be reasonable to assume that at least one of the other phases might represent the late fourteenth-century work that Emery stoutly maintained as a

date for the courtyard as a whole. It is possible that Emery's original opinion needs to be revised, and the South Court at Dartington contained different phases of work spreading throughout the later medieval centuries into the Tudor period. Emery's (1970, 192–5) dismissal of the late medieval/early Tudor period at Dartington, when it was owned by a series of high status owners (1476–1548; this includes Sir Thomas St Leger 1476–83, Margaret, countess of Richmond 1487–1509, Henry Courtenay, marquis of Exeter 1525–39, Queen Catherine Howard 1539–42 and Queen Catherine Parr 1542–8) as being a time when no building work was undertaken needs to be seriously reconsidered. Even if there is no proof that the last four mentioned were in permanent residence, there is no reason why the buildings should not have been expected to have been of a quality prepared to receive their visits. The evidence of the 1990s excavations seemed to suggest there was more activity in this period than Emery

Fig. 23 Dartington Hall (c.1870) showing the formal 'Dutch Garden' on the 'Tiltyard' floor. Note the church (demolished in the late nineteenth century) to the left of the hall

allowed. The ruined 'arches' on the lawn can now best be seen as dating from this period.

Excavation on the terraces proved to be disappointing. Evidence for the parterre on the 'Tiltyard' floor had been completely removed during the Elmhirst's ownership. On the Bowling Green a series of soil dumps were identified from the medieval period onwards. The east wall to the 'fine garden' was excavated, and dated to the late seventeenth or early eighteenth century. Occasional planting holes were recovered on its west side, suggesting espaliered fruit trees trained against the wall. Despite the wall being reduced to just above foundation height, at least two curious features were noted within it. One was a crude arch under the wall, the other was a possible small rustic alcove that may have held a wall plant of some sort. These features may have given the wall a deliberate air of antiquity. Coupled with the deliberate retention of the ruined arches, it seems that the late seventeenth/early eighteenth century gardens at Dartington were designed to reflect the old fashioned nature of the buildings. This might be seen as a prelude to the grander schemes for contrived anachronisms in the early nineteenth century, and Dartington might be seen as an early attempt to create an 'antiquarian' type garden.

Archaeology found much to support the idea that the valley floor had once held a pond, or, at least, some sort of feature connected with water. On the far side of the terraces a partly rock-cut tunnel was re-exposed leading from a stone conduit house behind the ancient chestnuts. This structure had no datable features. Conduit houses, for providing drinking water, were common features of larger medieval establishments. The only dating evidence was the line of the terraces, which clearly cut across the tunnel, truncating it. It is thought the tunnel was used as some sort of conduit to take water from the conduit house across the valley, possibly to the hall, but a medieval date can not be confirmed.

Another stone-lined drain of some size was found under the line of the first terrace. This carried a stream unseen through the 'Tiltyard' along the bottom of the southern edge of the terraces. It was set into the level of the Dutch Garden (Currie 1991–8). The Elmhirsts subsequently reduced the floor by another terrace leaving the stream to be channelled along a line above the 'Tiltyard' floor. This was further evidence that the level they assumed to be 'correct' was wrong. If the drain was contemporary with the square pond shown in 1805, it was probably a diversion channel taking the stream along the side of the pond to prevent silt being deposited therein, and to make draining the pond for cleaning relatively easy. This author has shown how diversion channels were common features associated with medieval and early post-medieval ponds (Currie 1988, 270–4).

Conclusions

Archaeology, aided by documentary research, has produced a new view of how the house and gardens at Dartington developed. Rather than trying to attribute the entire double-courtyard mansion to John Holand in the late fourteenth century, it now seems that the curiously unsymmetrical plan that emerges developed over a much wider date range. It is now confirmed that there was a substantial building phase in the later fifteenth and early sixteenth century, when the hall was part of the estates of a series of English queens.

The south courtyard was demolished before 1682, and replaced by a garden known as the 'fine garden'. This seems to have contained a series of seemingly odd features for a late seventeenth century garden, including a set of ruined arches, and a distinctive set of surrounding walls. It is possible that even at this early date an attempt was made to create an air of antiquity within the design that may in some ways, pre-empt the Gothic of the later eighteenth century. In the early nineteenth century grandiose schemes were put forward for rebuilding Dartington as an elaborate Gothic fantasy mansion. The first of these, in 1805, produced a series of plans and illustrations, which largely appear not to have mented.

The second attempt, in 1845, involved the Gothic Revivalist architect, Augustus Pugin. Although it never advanced beyond the rebuilding of the Solar wing in the house, it may have been responsible for creating the formal terraces in the valley below.

These are not recorded in 1805 or on the tithe map of 1839. There have been numerous attempts to explain away this as an omission. These researches suggest the omission may have been real, and that nothing was shown because nothing was there. It is suggested that the terraces were created at the time of Pugin's work on Dartington to further enhance the air of antiquity about the place. This was seemingly much treasured by the Champernowne family as a way of consistently illustrating their status as one of Devon's oldest landed families. The term 'antiquarian garden' is suggested to explain the curious nature of the Dartington garden's development. Although there are many such gardens that might be cited in the nineteenth century, the unusual feature of this site is that the deliberate attempt to invoke an atmosphere of antiquity began before 1682, and evolved over a much longer period that the more ordinary nineteenth-century formal revivalist garden.

References – Original Sources

At Dartington Hall:
The Dartington archive was not numbered at the time of the research. The designations given below were created by the author for identification in the text.

Tithe survey: Tithe Map of Dartington, 1839 in archive room.

Froude: Watercolour of south front by Archdeacon Froude, 1801, in toilet on first floor of private wing.

Garden/1: Photograph of Dutch Garden in Tilt-yard, undated but with pencil notes on back suggesting *c.*1864, in toilet on first floor of private wing.

Garden/2: Photograph of Dutch Garden in Tilt-yard, undated but probably *c.*1900, in bar of White Hart; reproduced on page 19 of Snell 1989 (see below).

In the Devon Record Office:
Z15/1/3 Deed of exchange, Polsloe Priory for Dartington Hall, 1559

Z15/38/1/22/2 Release & Quitclaim, 15th February 1682, Dartington Hall

Z15/38/1/7/1–23 Volume of plans and illustrations of Dartington Hall, late eighteenth/early nineteenth century

In the West Country Studies Library:
Ordnance Survey 25" plans, sheet 121.1 (1889 ed.)

Ordnance Survey 25" plans, sheet 121.1 (1904 ed.)

References – Secondary Sources

C. E. Champernowne, *unpublished typescript history of the Chapernowne family*, 1954

Currie, C. K. 1988 'Hampshire fishponds', M. Aston (ed.), *Medieval fish, fisheries and fishponds in England*, British Archaeological Reports no. 182, 2 vols, 1988, 267–89

Currie, C. K. 1991–1998 *Excavations in the gardens of Dartington Hall*, unpublished interim reports, copies in the Devon County Council Sites and Monuments Record, Exeter

Emery, A. 1958 'Dartington Hall, Devonshire', *Archaeol. J.*, 115 , 184–202

Emery, A. 1970 *Dartington Hall*

Emery, A. 1975 'Dartington Hall, Devonshire', M. J. Swanton (ed.), *Studies in Medieval Domestic Architecture*, 1975, 134–152

Hussey, C. 1938 'Dartington Hall, Devon part 1', *Country Life*, 27th August 1938; 'Dartington Hall, Devon part 2', *Country Life*', 3rd September 1938

Pevsner, N. 1952 *The buildings of England: South Devon*

Platt, C. 1962 'Excavations at Dartington Hall, 1962', *Archaeol. J.*, 119, (1962), 208–224

Snell, R. 1989 *From the bare stem. Making Dorothy Elmhirst's garden at Dartington Hall*

Post-Medieval Garden Features at Shilston Barton

Introduction

It is perhaps a curious coincidence that the steward employed by the Champernownes to carry out the unfinished attempt to rebuild Dartington Hall into a Gothic Revival mansion in 1805 was Christopher Savery. His family hailed from the Devon parish of Modbury, as did the earliest Champernownes. They must have had many connections, and it is interesting to note that there is a castellated Gothic arch leading into the farmyard at Shilston with a date stone '1819'. This same Christopher Savery had tried to persuade Arthur Champernowne not to remove the roof to Dartington Hall in 1813 (Champernowne 1954), and one might guess that he had an appreciation of Gothic architecture himself. There are at least three castellated Gothic garden buildings in the landscape of his own estate at Shilston, and it is possible his work at Dartington had some influence on his own property.

The history of Shilston extends, like Dartington, back to Domesday and beyond. It is

perhaps another coincidence that a conjectured picture of the ancient family manor house has a hall and porch remarkably similar to that at Dartington (Modbury Local History Society 1980, 5). This building seems to have been demolished, possibly *c.*1700. It is not known what the second mansion at Shilston looked like. This is because around 1813, the year that the Champernownes removed the Dartington Hall roof, their steward, Christopher Savery, is reputed to have rebuilt Shilston for a third time, probably producing the current house, Shilston Barton (Lysons & Lysons 1822, 6.ii, 343; WCSL Sale Particulars, Modbury Parish Folder).

Garden Remains at Shilston Barton

Shilston Barton, at the time of the work here under discussion, was a poor reflection of the great houses that once stood on the site. The property had been owned by the Saverys since 1614 (Polwhele 1793–1806, 462). Before that it had been in the hands of the Hill family since at least 1392–3 (Pearse Chope 1967, 59n). Although the Saverys had once been a family of great influence in the county, they gradually lost

Fig. 24 Shilston Barton (from the south) in the summer of 2000. The three arch façade to the grotto is at the head of the valley
(© Christopher Currie)

Fig. 25 Shilston Barton. The grotto from the south, with the pond in the foreground and the Barton farmhouse behind the grotto (© Christopher Currie)

Fig. 26 The interior of the grotto, showing the rear wall of the central compartment, part of the original 'water theatre'. The water from the stone basin in the alcove leaves via a hole between the 'legs' on the left side of the basin (© Christopher Currie)

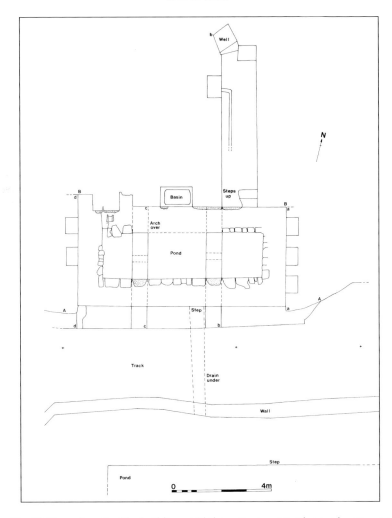

Fig. 27 Plan of grotto-like building at Shilston Barton (© Christopher Currie)

interest in Shilston in the later eighteenth and early nineteenth centuries, moving their favoured residence elsewhere. The third house declined into use as a farmstead, a situation mirrored at Dartington, where the medieval north court became the barton farmyard. The gardens that once decorated the earlier houses became largely forgotten and overgrown. A recent purchase of the property by Sebastian Fenwick led to a revived interest in these derelict features, and many new discoveries have been made that reveal an extensive designed landscape. Activity by Mr Fenwick has revealed at least two separate sets of terracing, three ponds with the remains of ornamental rills and a cascade, and a

previous unknown castellated eyecatcher. This adds to the fine walled garden already known about. The most exciting discovery, however, was reserved for a curious triple arched structure at the head of the uppermost pond. This had remained partly buried until recently. Having begun digging it out, its unusual nature suggested that the remainder of the excavations should be done under archaeological scrutiny. Following this decision, the present author was called in to try to make sense of what proved to be a remarkable structure.

It is not proposed to go into the detailed documentary research that supports the provisional conclusions that have been reached about

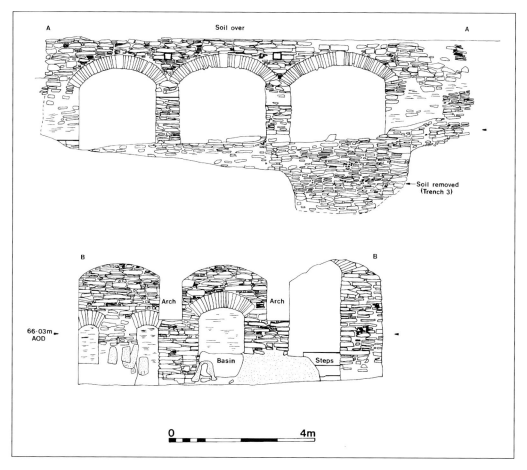

Fig. 28 Front and rear elevations of grotto-like building at Shilston (© Christopher Currie). A-A Front elevation (south facing). B-B Rear elevation (south facing). See plan for location of elevations

this building. Suffice to say it is now thought that its discovery makes it a structure of more than local importance to the county of Devon. It is possible that it could be a unique survival of a garden ornament that was much talked about around the turn of the seventeenth and eighteenth centuries, but of which no certain example is known to the author to have survived within the United Kingdom.

The Shilston Water Theatre

No attempt will be made here to give a detailed description of the triple arched structure at Shilston. Readers interested in greater detail

should refer to a fuller report by this author (Currie 2000). It was clearly a highly complex building that contains a large number of recesses, alcoves and water-related features. The building comprises a spring-fed well set at the back of a tunnel that was cut into the hillside below the house. This is similar to a small number of other tunnel-grottoes being created in England in the late seventeenth century, and they have some similarities to earlier medieval 'holy wells' (*ibid.*). Originally it appears that there was a terrace wall through which the tunnel was cut. Set into this wall are a series of alcoves, a basin, and a number of outlets from which water, collected from springs in the hillside behind, could be made to pour. Before this wall was a small rectangular basin, and two stone steps down into the main pond at the top of the valley. In its heyday the play of water from the outlets in this wall would have been most entertaining. One of the exits for water appears to be between the legs of a carved figure, possible a Pan or a Sheila-na-gig, but such is the erosion to the structure it is no longer possible to tell exactly what it was originally.

Such plays of water were well known in Italian Renaissance gardens. Stephen Switzer shows many illustrations of them in his 1729 book, *A universal system of water and waterworks, philosophical and practical*, a treatise on ornamental water features for gardens. They were commonly known as 'water theatres' by contemporaries. There are no known extant examples of such 'theatres' in the United Kingdom. Horace Walpole wrote in the later eighteenth century how the complex hydrological ornaments in earlier formal gardens had to be abandoned because of their costly maintenance. He states that:

> *But for magnitude and enormous cost, the hydraulic works, fountains and waterfalls, were the most extraordinary; indeed, their extreme first expense, and the constant demand for supporting them in perfection, led in a few years to their total disuse. Neglect soon occasioned decay, and decay caused their entire removal.*
>
> (Wornum 1876, 97)

The Shilston example only seems to have survived because it was incorporated into a later triple arched grotto, which has protected it from the elements. Probable use of the grotto as a cold store or butter-well when the Shilston estate was a farmstead has further helped save this unusual structure.

It is not possible to give exact dates for either phase of this building. The water theatre may date from around the time the mansion was rebuilt for the first time in *c.*1700, although it could easily be earlier. In the reigns of William and Mary the Saverys had been much favoured

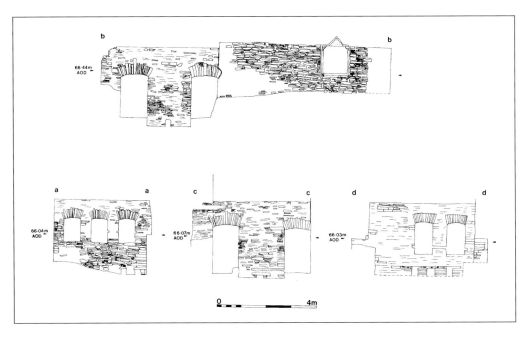

Fig. 29 Shilston internal elevations of grotto-like building (© Christopher Currie). a-a internal east wall, west facing elevation. b-b internal wall to spring head, east facing. c-c internal wall, east facing. d-d internal west wall, east facing elevation

as supporters of the Protestant settlement, and it is possible that the creation of an elaborate garden coincided with their rise in fortune. The conversion of the water theatre into full-scale grotto is likewise undateable. Stylistically, triple arched features were very popular between *c.*1720 and 1750. This type of frontage was common around that time, and can be seen in designs of William Kent at well-known gardens at Rousham, Chiswick and Claremont. However, there appears to have been work undertaken on the estate between 1813–19 that might account for the change. As we have seen at Dartington, it is all to easy to mistake early nineteenth century formal revivalist features with earlier work, and the Christopher Savery who rebuilt the Shilston house for the second time was deeply involved with a revivalist project at Dartington.

Regardless of the dates of the two phases in the grotto building at Shilston, it has to be considered an exceptional example of its kind, and is perhaps unique in the United Kingdom in so clearly demonstrating two important stages in grotto development.

References – Original Sources

In the West Country Studies Library
Modbury Parish Folder, folder of newspaper cuttings and other material on Modbury. This includes copies of sale advertisements for Shilston Barton for 6th August 1818 and 14th June 1821.

Original sources in print
Pearse Chope, R. (ed.) 1967 *Early Tours in Devon and Cornwall* (reprinted from first edition of 1918)

Switzer, S. 1729 *A universal system of water and water-works, philosophical and practical*, 2 vols

Walpole, H. 1876 'A history of modern taste in gardening', *Anecdotes of painting in England*, (1876, ed. R. N. Wornum)

Secondary sources
Currie, C. K. 2000 'Archaeological recording of garden features at Shilston Barton, Modbury, Devon' unpublished report to South Hams District Council and Sebastian Fenwick (publicly accessible copies in the Devon County Council SMR at Exeter, and the NMR)

Lysons, D. & Lysons, S. 1822 *Magna Britannia. Volume 6 part II, Devon*

Modbury Local History Society, *Modbury. Our inheritance*, Plymouth, 1980

Polwhele, R. *The History of Devonshire*, 3 vols, 1793–1806

Garden Archaeology in South Devon

Robert Waterhouse

Introduction

The two designed landscapes and their gardens described below were identified during research for an MPhil at Exeter University, researching the origins and development of courtyard mansions in South Devon in the period from *c.*1200 – *c.*1650.

The geographical area covered by the study includes the whole of South Hams District, the environs of Plymouth and Teignbridge District to the south-west of the Haldon ridge. Of 41 houses so far visited, 17 have evidence for pre-eighteenth century gardens. The majority of these gardens are of the multiple terraced variety, laid out on an axis, alongside or facing a courtyard mansion. Of these, eight lie alongside the house, while of the others, two have water gardens and one is behind, but at right angles to the house. The other six are in line with their houses, all but one being to the rear. Fifteen of these sites are briefly described in a gazetteer at the end of this paper.

Two of the sites, not previously recorded, are of sufficient interest and complexity to merit detailed description. These are at Keynedon, in Sherford parish and Painsford, in Ashprington parish, both in South Hams District.

Keynedon Barton

Keynedon Barton is located in a shallow valley about 1km south of Sherford hamlet, close to the medieval road connecting Sherford to Frogmore Creek, a tidal arm of the Kingsbridge Estuary. This road runs along the eastern side of the level valley floor and passes through the designed landscape to be discussed. A substantial house and its outbuildings, grouped around three courtyards, is terraced into the steeply sloping west side of the valley, facing east. These buildings have been surveyed and interpreted, and were found to have developed during the period *c.*1300 – *c.*1622 from a scattered plan of Anglo-Norman type (Impey 1999, 68–70), to a complex mock-defensive mansion by the early sixteenth century (Waterhouse 2000, 127–200).

A designed landscape was laid out fronting this house, the earliest part of which comprised two ponds forming a sheet of water fronting the house, possibly dating from the early sixteenth century. Later developments include a formal garden in the outer courtyard of *c.*1596, and the creation of a small terraced formal garden east of the road in the early seventeenth century.

The Early Sixteenth Century Mock Moat

The approach to Keynedon Barton in the early sixteenth century was staged and dramatic, providing the framework for subsequent embel-lishments in the later sixteenth century. From the mid to late fifteenth century, the house had a simple outer courtyard, flanked by agricultural buildings and closed at the front by a plain stone wall. This was removed and replaced in the early sixteenth century by a heavy stone wall, topped by a rampart walk. A small two storey gatehouse was placed off-centre in the wall, aligned on the front door of the house, also rebuilt at this time. It is uncertain whether the two large fishponds which occupy the valley floor outside this wall were newly dug in the early sixteenth century, or are developments of medieval ones. However, the dam for the upper pond is aligned on the gatehouse and carries a roadway which gave access to the house from the public road. The approach was thus

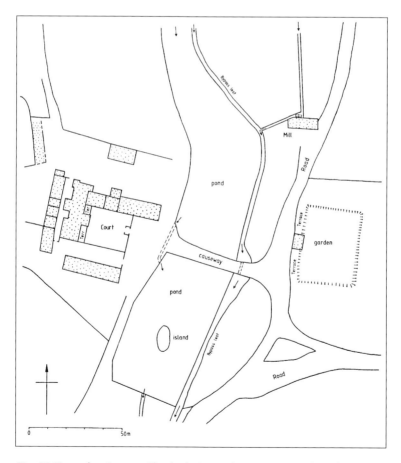

Fig. 30 Keynedon Barton, Sherford. General arrangement plan of buildings with locations of garden and water features (© Robert Waterhouse)

contrived as a causeway leading straight to the gatehouse and flanked by broad sheets of water.

The ponds are well engineered, with bypass leats along their eastern sides and a culvert linking the two, ensuring a slow flow through the ponds, while the silt brought down the valley by the stream was kept away from them via the side leats. This would create the right conditions for fish farming, those of slow-moving silt free water.

The Late Sixteenth Century Courtyard Garden

In 1596, the outer courtyard was remodelled, being divided from the large threshing barn to the south by a tall crenellated wall. This stepped up over a raised terrace, constructed along the front of the house and accessed from doors on either side of a tall crenellated porch. This porch was reached via a long flight of stone steps from the courtyard. Crenellations were also added to the front curtain wall, the wall-walk being accessed at the south east corner by a timber stair against the new dividing wall. A second arch was cut in the curtain wall to the south, giving access to the threshing barn, and a date-stone placed above to record the new work, bearing the arms of Richard Hals and his wife Jane Fortescue with the date 1596.

The terraces on either side of the porch suggest that the courtyard may have been converted into a formal garden surrounding the path from the gatehouse to the house. Parallels for this arrangement are discussed below.

The Early Seventeenth Century Terraced Garden

A sub-rectangular level area in the field to the east of the road, opposite the entrance to the house, may be the site of a second formal

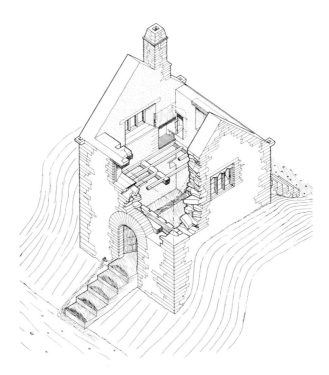

Fig. 31 Roadside elevation of 'The Laundry', a possible pleasure house at Keynedon Barton. Note large first floor windows, fireplace and associated food warmer, with water flowing through unlit cellar below (© Robert Waterhouse)

garden, possibly with a central water feature, fed by a stream which flows out of a short side valley to the east. A broad raised terrace ran alongside, dividing this level area from the road. A small two storey stone building stands in the centre of this terrace and is reconstructed in figures 31 and 32. Known locally as The Laundry, it appears to have given access from the road into the possible garden. The terrace abuts the side walls of the building. The ground floor room is thus partly underground and seems to have functioned as a cold-store, with cupboards in the walls and a stream of water running across the floor and passing out of a spout in the front wall. Suggestions for its use have included a dairy, but these are normally single storied and found close to the house. The building's first floor room was reached by an external flight of steps at the south-east corner and had a domestic fireplace, a food-warming alcove and four large windows. These would have given views of the possible garden to the east,

the terraces to north and south, and a dramatic view of the castellated mansion across the valley to the west, reflected in its fishponds. On the east side of the building was a small mounting block. Study of the field patterns in the area immediately to the east suggests the presence of a former riding or coursing park of about 120 acres. This park is wedge shaped, with a narrow rectangular field at the western extremity. As the 'Laundry' stands at the western end of this field, it is possible that it may have served as a standing for viewing the hunt. This may even offer an alternative explanation of the building's name – a 'Laund' being a medieval term for a treeless area within a park (Rackham 1995, 155–7).

Notwithstanding the possible presence of a park, it is suggested that the building was a pleasure house, contained within and overlooking a formal garden, with the fishponds being treated as a water garden to reflect views of the mansion (see comments on Ilton Castle

Fig. 32 Rear elevation of 'The Laundry', Keynedon Barton, with stair to first floor and covered water channel to cellar. Note broad bank against side walls, possibly carrying a terrace walk (© Robert Waterhouse)

in gazetteer). The fireplace with food warmer and cold-store below suggest that the building could also have been used as a small banqueting house. Its modern name may alternatively suggest that the water supply may have suited its conversion to a laundry at a later date. The house and its outbuildings are listed grade II*, but the possible pleasure house is not at present listed.

Historical Background

Keynedon was held in fee by several absentee landlords until about 1300, when a local minor gentry family, the Pralls, who had owned the farm for some time, made it their seat. The farm was probably given in marriage about 1370 to another local family, that of Govy. John Govy was granted a licence for a chapel in 1409, but had died by 1412, when his widow Agnes married John Hals, then a magistrate on the King's Bench in London, later to become Justice of the Common Pleas. He never lived at Keynedon, but his son Richard, who inherited in 1434, was certainly living at Keynedon from the 1450s, when he was MP for Plympton and Sheriff of Devon. The Hals family remained there until the 1640s, when they moved their seat to Efford, near Eggbuckland. Richard Hals, the sixth descendent from John, was imprisoned for debts in 1622 and there is ample evidence for expensive alterations to the house in the first quarter of the seventeenth century. This must include the pleasure house, its garden and possible park, while Richard's father, who was responsible for the 1596 outer courtyard reconstruction, may have passed on old debts.

The Hals family held Keynedon until 1684, but did not live there after the 1640s. It subsequently passed through various families, but except for a short period in the early nineteenth century, it has remained a tenanted farm. The ponds remained in water until the early twentieth century but are now silted up and partly filled in. The outer court of the house is mainly under tarmacadam, but substantial remains of its enclosing walls and the porch remain. The pleasure house currently serves as an animal shelter with hayloft over, and a pasture on the possible garden site to its east.

Painsford Manor

Painsford Manor lies about 1km south-west of Ashprington village on the north bank of the Harbourne valley, the river meandering across its floodplain 250m to the south. The house, which has been surveyed and interpreted (Waterhouse, forthcoming), sits on a man-made terrace about 20m up the valley side and originally faced a medieval road to its north. An outer walled courtyard contains a late seventeenth-century stable block. A second, inner courtyard has a detached chapel, licenced in 1400 and a possible thirteenth to fourteenth century detached chamber-block. A kitchen of fifteenth-century date stood to the rear, later forming a projecting wing on the south east corner of the house. A second wing was built to complement it in the early seventeenth century; this is described below. The gardens are of two periods, the first being late sixteenth to early seventeenth century, the second from between *c.*1670–1710.

The Early Seventeenth Century Loggia

The first period is characterised by the creation of a square formal garden on the west side of the house. This was complemented by a two storey loggia wing which projected to the rear of the house from its south west corner, balancing the kitchen wing, already in existence to the east (Fig. 34). This loggia represents one of the most spectacular garden-related structures in Devon, yet is surprisingly little known. It was built in slate ashlar, its arcaded loggia facing into the courtyard to its east and an integral wall enclosing the courtyard on its south side. The space thus enclosed may therefore have contained a formal garden, with the house on its north, the kitchen on the east and the elegant octagonal pillars and chamfered

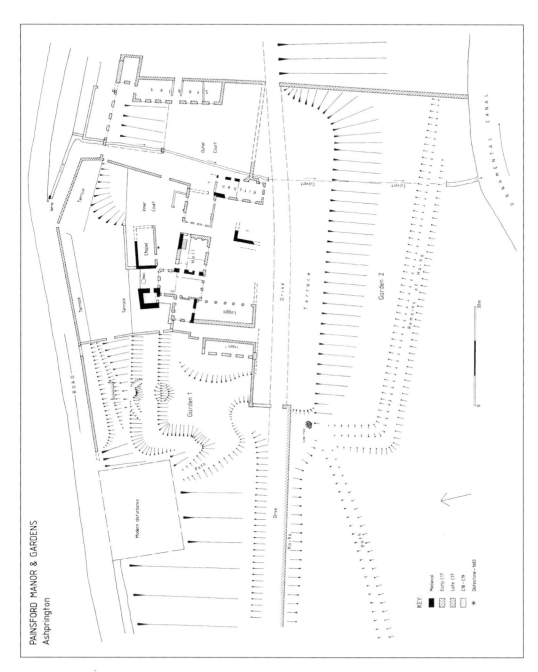

Fig. 33 Painsford Manor, Ashprington. General arrangement plan of buildings with locations of garden and landscape features (© Robert Waterhouse)

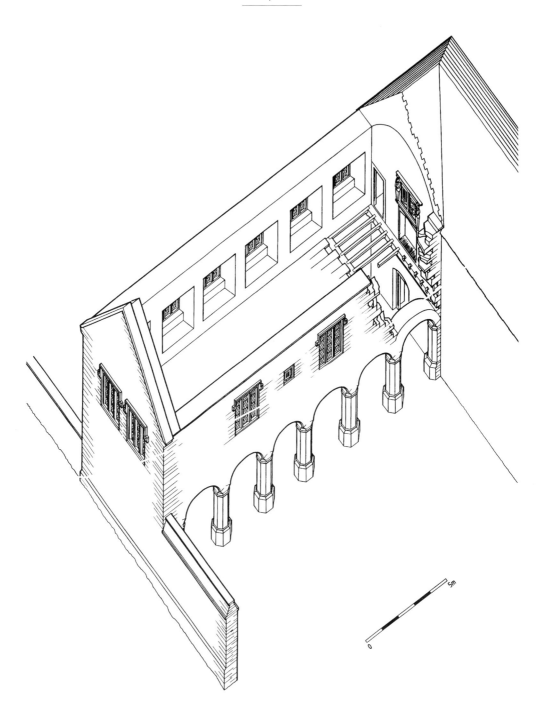

Fig. 34 Painsford Manor. Early seventeenth century loggia, surmounted by a long gallery, projecting from parlour of hall range. This structure may have been built after the marriage of Samuel Somaster of Painsford to Frances Strode in 1607. It faced into a small courtyard garden and overlooked a terraced formal garden to the rear (© Robert Waterhouse)

shallow arches of the loggia to its west. The south and west walls of the loggia were windowless although at its north end a door gave access to the parlour of the house.

Masonry survival at first floor level is very fragmentary, but enough remains to show that there was a long gallery, entered from the house, with a Beer stone fireplace at its north end and at least one large window, possibly two, in the south gable. Long galleries usually had many windows along both sides, but as none survive at Painsford the design of these has been assumed. A pair of early seventeenth-century oak caryatids found recently in the house may have belonged to an overmantel above the fireplace. They have been loaned to Totnes Museum.

The Late Seventeenth Century Grand Front and Ornamental Landscape

The late seventeenth-century garden is of a much larger scale. West of the loggia and aligned with it, and therefore overlooked by the long gallery, are the earthworks of a square formal garden, terraced on two sides into the hillside. Three terraces survive on the north side, tailing off with the slope to two on the west. A disturbance, central to the north side, suggests a flight of steps leading up the terraces to a small stone structure, possibly a gazebo, on the upper terrace. A stone wall shields the garden from the road; this continues to the east to the main gate into the early seventeenth century outer courtyard. A further stone wall contains the south side of the garden, but this is fragmentary.

In about 1680, the central rooms of the house were expanded by extending them to the south and lining them with richly moulded panelling. The house frontage was turned around from the north to the south and the expanded house with its projecting wings became the centre point of a semi-formal, semi-landscape garden which was laid out to the south. The new frontage was accessed by drives which diverged from the road about 200m to the east and west. These were walled on their north sides, with ha-has to the south. The wall along the south side of the southern courtyard was demolished, the

former court becoming a turning area for carriages. To its south, a broad terrace was flanked by a pair of lime trees, one of which survives. This terrace falls steeply to a narrow rectangular terrace, surrounded by the ha-ha, and overlooking a gentle slope down to an ornamental canal, which doubles as the storage pond for Painsford Mill, a short distance to the east.

A path, still a public right of way, led along the south side of this canal. A stand of lime trees flanked the view to the west, perhaps complemented by another to the east, now gone.

It is not certain how far the park-like landscape extended, though large trees stand in clumps across the steep southern side of the Harbourne valley, suggesting that the grounds were once extensive. Although a ha-ha is present, no licence for a deer park is recorded. This is perhaps surprising, given the social status of the owners in the late seventeenth century (see below).

Further terraced gardens immediately north of the house may also date from this period. Here there is a narrow terrace where fruit trees grew, overlooking a broad terrace, raised above the house and probably for domestic use. This, the former front of the house, has been subjected to major earth moving, substantially changing the character of this area.

A large kitchen garden on the hillside to the north-west of the house and road was only walled on its west and north, presumably the only directions from which the prevailing wind was a problem. The north wall is buttressed at equal intervals. Lower Washbourne Barton, 1km to the south (*qv*) which may also have been owned by the Kellands, has a semi-walled garden of similar design, in an identical position.

Fragments of Beer stone, now in a neighbouring house, but known to have come from Painsford, include a pair of grotesque bearded heads forming the keystones of segmental arches. These appear to be late seventeenth or early eighteenth century and offer a tantalising glimpse of a lost building, perhaps in the parkland landscape south of the mansion.

The house and loggia at Painsford are listed grade II*, while the south east kitchen wing and stable block are grade II. A stone bridge, which apparently led to a warren, again probably of late seventeenth century or early eighteenth-century date, is also listed grade II.

Historical Background

Painsford's early history is unknown, but the farm was owned by a minor gentry family, the Peperells, in the early fifteenth century, the male line dying out *c.*1430. The heiress Alice Peperell then married Walter Halwell, whose family sold out to the mercantile Somaster family in about 1505. The Somasters, who may have originated on the continent, held Painsford until 1650, when the property passed by marriage to John Kelland, who was Sheriff of Devon in 1665, as was his son John in 1683. The male line died out in 1710 and the middle-aged heiresses then let out the property to tenant farmers. It is not certain what happened subsequently, but the carriage drives, loggia and canal were certainly still recognisable in 1780, when an illustration was made of them in sale particulars of the estate (Gray 1995, 174). The house was modified *c.*1800 as the residence of a gentleman farmer, with many large farm buildings constructed on a new site to the north. It has remained a farmhouse, resulting in the preservation of the loggia as a romantic ruin, in its current condition from at least 1840 (Gray

1995, 175); the relict gardens lying within an orchard to the west and rough pasture to the south.

Discussion

The two sites described above developed in contrasting ways over several generations. It is difficult, owing to the paucity of examples, to draw blanket assumptions as to trends in garden development in the district, but certain observations can be made.

The identification of several other relict gardens, listed below, assists in identifying these trends and helps to identify typical features of early gardens in South Devon. Two main periods of construction can be identified. The first, in the late sixteenth to early seventeenth century, can be related to the prosperous and peaceful late Tudor to early Stuart period, when house construction projects were common among gentry and noble families (Airs 1995, 3–22). The second period coincides with the resurgence of building and other expressions of wealth and status after the Restoration of Charles II in 1660. This period began with

Fig. 35 Painsford garden terraces (© Robert Waterhouse)

much experimentation in garden design and landscape settings, and culminated in the development of the classic ornamental parkland which surrounded many great houses by the mid-eighteenth century.

An interesting feature of these discoveries is that they have been made in an area which has not been traditionally associated with early gardens. The only early formal gardens previously known in South Devon are those at Dartington Hall, just outside Totnes, and Langdon Court, near Wembury. The former was thought to be a fourteenth-century tiltyard (Emery 1970, 10–11) and has only recently been re-identified as having late-seventeenth and mid nineteenth-century phases (Currie, this volume), while the well-preserved late seventeenth-century formal gardens at Langdon Court are little known. These new discoveries combine to show that South Devon has a garden heritage to compare with the rest of southern England, and one that has previously been unknown.

Referring now to the two gardens described in detail, the first site at Keynedon Barton is remarkable for its water features. The placing of ponds fronting a house, bisected by an access causeway, is unusual in south-west England, whereas it is a relatively common feature of Breton manoirs (Meirion-Jones 1993, 175). Other gentry houses in Devon have evidence for the channelling of streams along their frontages, especially where a curtain wall and gatehouse are present, but the use of large ponds is rare. Fishponds as an adjunct to manor houses are common, not to say essential to the running of a large household, but their use in architectural display is unusual. The use of large lakes to reflect castles is known from the medieval period, with extensive water defences at Kenilworth Castle, Warwickshire, dating from the twelfth century. These were used in 1575 to entertain Elizabeth I, with mock sea battles being performed. Large ponds were also used as features within a pleasure garden, laid out between 1550 and 1646 by the Earls of Worcester, surrounding Raglan Castle in Gwent (Whittle 1989, 88–89).

The use of ponds as water features within gardens is less rare. The Bishop's Palace at Wells, Somerset, is claimed to have used natural pools above its hot springs as decorative features within the private gardens of the Bishop. At Bodiam Castle, Sussex, ponds and earthwork features are considered to belong to extensive water gardens surrounding the late fourteenth century castle (Taylor, C., Everson, P. and Wilson-North, R. 1990).

In Devon, two large fishponds within the deer park at Berry Pomeroy were overlooked by the late fifteenth to early seventeenth century castle and may have been part of a designed landscape in its immediate vicinity (Brown 1999, 36–41). The use of enclosed courtyards as formal gardens, with associated buildings used as focus structures, seen at Keynedon and Painsford, is interesting, if only in the potential it has for many other sites. Local parallels are not known, but in about 1597, a formal garden was laid out in the base court of Prince Mauritz of Orange's urban mansion at The Hague (Cremers 1973, 14).

The use of specialist function buildings such as banqueting houses within gardens is less rare, a good example being Campden House, Chipping Campden, Gloucestershire, where paired banqueting houses overlooking either end of a raised terrace walk were constructed between 1609 and 1629 (Everson 1989, 109–121). These invite comparison with the probable banqueting house at Keynedon, flanked by terraced walks and overlooking other designed features.

Locations of the other examples listed below, where gardens can be seen to relate directly to buildings include Gatcombe House, Littlehempston, where a small triple terraced garden is aligned on a ballroom of c.1690, and Langdon Court, Wembury, where two gazebos of similar date occupy corners of a lawn facing the house. It would appear that only the largest and most complex of gardens have buildings designed to overlook them, such as the long galleries at Painsford and Dartington and the pleasure house at Keynedon, while isolated structures within gardens are found in both periods of garden creation. It may be possible to say that of these, sites of the earlier Tudor/Stuart period can possess buildings related only to the gardens, while detached buildings which are designed to relate to the house can only be found in gardens of the later period. This can only be advanced as a tentative suggestion however, given the few examples on which this theory is based.

The buildings belong to classes of structure on which little has been written. Long galleries and loggias have been noted as features of several English houses of the late sixteenth to early seventeenth centuries, the idea having been imported from France in the late fifteenth century. These have consistently been discussed in their architectural context with little reference to the visual aspect of their design, especially in relation to the gardens and landscapes which they overlooked.

Buildings of similar design to the loggia/long gallery at Painsford are known from a few sites in the West Country. Examples include an early seventeenth-century two storied link range supported on pillars at Godolphin Hall, Cornwall and a single storey arcaded verandah, possibly of a similar date, at Horton Court, Gloucestershire, but neither of these have been published in detail. A single storey loggia within a crenellated outer courtyard, recorded in an early eighteenth-century illustration of Bowhill House, Exeter was recently identified by Stuart Blaylock (Blaylock, forthcoming). A fragmentary example, probably two storied, was observed during late nineteenth-century alterations at the courtyard mansion of North Wyke, North Tawton (Lega-Weekes 1900, 198). A fragmentary arcaded structure on the south side of the inner court of Dartington Hall is claimed to be part of a ground floor long gallery dating from the late fourteenth century (Emery 1970, 187–191), but this has recently had an early sixteenth-century date suggested for it (Currie 1999, 25). Direct comparisons can, however, be made with buildings in Totnes, which share with Painsford the slate voussoired arches supported on pillars. These are No. 16 High Street, dating from 1585, and the former market hall opposite (now demolished) of about 1610.

Long galleries and loggias, despite origins in France in the late fifteenth century, are claimed by R. Coope (1986, 51–53) to have been most popular in England between *c.*1550 and *c.*1625. She notes that a pair of galleries on either side

of a gatehouse at Buckhurst, Kent, drawn by the Elizabethan architect John Thorpe, were noted as being "for ye Ladye syde" and "for my Lord's syde", an arrangement strongly reminiscent of the raised terraces either side of the porch at Keynedon, probably overlooking an enclosed garden.

Gardens in South Devon belonging to the later period, from the Restoration until the mid-eighteenth century, can be split into two groups. In the early part of the period, they seem to have followed the traditions of the period before the Civil War, and were relatively small, with formal planting or lawns on multiple terracing, sometimes incorporating water features, dependent on location.

By about 1690 they had expanded in scale, and at some sites, e.g.: Painsford and possibly Follaton, small ornamental parks lay outside symmetrical terraced gardens, positioned on the same axis as the house. Painsford has evidence for such development in its planted groups and solitary lime trees. Its ha-has, apparently of this period, are of considerable interest, as the earliest known ha-ha, at Althorp, Gloucestershire, may date from the 1680s (Fletcher 1991, 153).

Walled ornamental deer parks are less common. Local examples include Boringdon of 1699 and Flete, probably of the early eighteenth century, while an example at Dartington on the site of a larger medieval park has recently been shown to have been re-enclosed in 1738 (Veryan Heal, personal communication). It contained carefully located plantations, one of which had long wings, flanking a small pleasure house on a prominent hilltop, while a long carriage drive from Totnes to Dartington Hall passed through the park beside the River Dart (Heal & Waterhouse, forthcoming). Similar woodland wings were planted on either side of a lodge at Lodge Park, Gloucestershire in 1733 (Fretwell 1995, 138–140).

The role of medieval and post-medieval deer parks has been lightly touched upon here, with the study of Cornish deer parks forming the subject of a separate paper (Herring, this volume). Several deer parks have been identified through the study of courtyard mansions in South Devon. These will form the basis of a future article (Waterhouse, forthcoming), although where a deer park is associated with a particular site described in the gazetteer below, it is mentioned.

Gazetteer

Alston, Malborough.

Alston, a small farmhouse with medieval origins, was greatly expanded during the eighteenth and early nineteenth centuries. The house, which has been surveyed and interpreted (Waterhouse, forthcoming) had a terraced garden, entered via a gateway opposite its southern, secondary frontage. The garden comprises two narrow upper terraces, now vegetable gardens, revetted and surrounded by walls of small locally-made bricks of the early eighteenth century. Two broader terraces below were enclosed by cob walls and are now grassed, containing an orchard. A central disturbance in the scarp between these two terraces suggests the former existence of a flight of steps.

The use of brick in a rural context at this date is very unusual in Devon (Beacham 1990, 27), a distinction shared with the late seventeenth-century gardens at Langdon Court, Wembury (see below).

Boringdon Hall, Plympton St Mary

This large, E plan early seventeenth-century house, now an hotel, is sited on a terrace in a south facing hillside, 2km north of Plympton. Remains of a formal garden laid out on five terraces west of the house and aligned north to south, survive as earthworks. The lowest and largest pair of terraces are now a car-park and tennis court, but the upper terraces are visible as narrower earthworks in the lawn to the north-west of the hotel. A nineteenth-century water cistern and a twentieth-century putting green have disturbed this area, but it is still possible to identify the terraces on the closely mown lawn surrounding the hotel.

A 220 acre deer park to the north west was licenced to George Parker of Boringdon in 1699 and substantial earthworks of its pale are preserved in Boringdon Park Wood. A rabbit warren lay between the house and park. A large triumphal arch designed by Robert Adam in 1783 lies just outside the park to its south west and was intended to be an eyecatcher from the dining room of Saltram House. This is listed grade II*, but is currently in poor condition.

Dartington Hall

On the south side of the inner courtyard of this large medieval house, an arcaded long gallery probably of early sixteenth-century date, originally overlooked a natural combe. A large three-sided terraced garden was later fitted into this combe. This is described in more detail by Currie (this volume).

Recent survey work has shown that a large deer park existed in the medieval period beside the River Dart to the north. To the north west was an empaled wood of about 90 acres, known since at least the sixteenth century as North Wood. This is probably the park which was stocked with deer by 1325 and described in 1550 as a chase, for hunting on horseback. A separate enclosed area of up to 76 acres was emparked to the east, and contained a free-standing lodge. An additional wooded chase and open park area was added on its west, possibly in 1413, creating an enclosed area of about 315 acres. Two medieval lodges may have been located within the park. Staverton Ford Plantation contains a substantial circular earthwork, containing a large rectangular stone building within a circular walled enclosure. This is tentatively identified as a 'standing' from which arranged hunts were watched from a viewing platform or first floor room (Waterhouse, forthcoming). This may date to the period between *c.*1388 and 1400, when Dartington was owned by John Holand, Duke of Huntingdon and Exeter, although a record of a later owner of the estate, Sir Arthur Champernowne, designing a banqueting house on an island in a lake at Antony in Cornwall cannot be ignored (Emery 1970, 42–43, 74).

In the southern part of the park, a number of 'court' fieldnames imply the former existence of a group of buildings. A low rectangular earthwork platform in fields to the north of Parsonage Farm may represent the site, possibly a second lodge. This may have been located near a gate in the park pale, indicated by 'postern' fieldnames in the vicinity. The medieval parsonage of Dartington, a small courtyard mansion of fourteenth to sixteenth century date, lies a short distance to the south-west.

Most of the park was disparked by 1550, but the early chase in North Wood was retained with a long narrow strip of land called the Newground added to the south east side of North Wood. This may have been used as a deercourse, where deer were driven by hounds down to one end to be shot. This has clear parallels with Lodge Park, Gloucestershire, where a similar deercourse is claimed by Fretwell (1995, 136–37) to date from the 1630s and at Keynedon Barton, as described above. The earliest of these courses known is that built by Henry VIII at Hampton Court in 1537, while an example at Godolphin Hall, Cornwall probably dates from the early seventeenth century.

The eastern part of Dartington Park was re-enclosed with a stone wall in 1738, covering 76 acres (see above). An eighteenth-century pleasure or summer house on a hilltop facing the Hall, is illustrated in a watercolour of 1801 by Rev. John Swete (DRO, 564M/F2/209), and has been incorporated into a modern house. This picture clearly shows the carriage drive meandering through the park alongside the River Dart.

Follaton House, Totnes

This Domesday manor was surrounded by a ha-ha of unknown, but possibly seventeenth-century date. This survives as a substantial earthwork to the south-east of the present, early nineteenth-century house, originally enclosing an area of about 50 acres around the house and designed to prevent stock from entering. To the south of the house, a combe contains a large garden on two broad terraces, flanked by pairs

of narrow terraces in the valley sides. This scheme predates the landscaped surroundings of the early nineteenth-century house and may have lain to the rear of an earlier house. An arched culvert which passes beneath the later house is aligned on the centre of the gardens and suggests that water features were present, fed by the stream which flows out of the combe. Precise dating evidence is not present, but the garden certainly pre-dates the present house.

Forde House, Newton Abbot

Forde House was built *c*.1550 by John Gaverock, an Exeter merchant, on the site of an earlier manor house, previously owned by Torre Abbey. The present E plan house dates to *c*.1610, with alterations in *c*.1625 in advance of a visit by Charles I.

Archaeological observations in Forde House grounds in 1998 found that the lawn to the south of the house had been laid out as a series of three long and shallow terraces at right angles to the frontage. Parch marks and faint earthworks suggest long bedding trenches, lined up on the porch at the centre of the house and possibly flanking a drive, predating *c*.1803 (Waterhouse 1998). A large fishpond along one side of this garden may belong to the earlier manor house.

Gatcombe House, Littlehempston

This double courtyard house, much altered in the nineteenth century, was occupied by the Bogan family of Totnes merchants during the sixteenth and seventeenth centuries. In about 1690, a large square ballroom was placed centrally in the hall range and probable service buildings around the inner courtyard were demolished to make way for a series of four small garden terraces, aligned on the ballroom.

Holcombe Burnell Barton

This small U plan manor house, built by the Dennis family in the late sixteenth to early seventeenth century, has a complex system of terraces, surrounding the building and descending the valley side to the north, where two long fishponds may have been re-used as landscape features. These terraces are interpreted as gardens constructed to complement the house. Holcombe Burnell Barton lies on the crest of a ridge, giving extensive views over a large deer park of *c*.400 acres, in existence by 1610. Its location within the park suggests that, like Berry Pomeroy Castle (Brown 1996, 13–14), Holcombe Burnell Barton may have been built on the site of an earlier hunting lodge.

Ilton Castle, Malborough

A quadrangular castle, licenced in 1337 to Sir John de Cheverston, was located here on the north side of a shallow valley. After his death, the manor of Ilton or Ithelstone passed to the Courtenay family, who held it until the nineteenth century. The site is a scheduled ancient monument, and includes part of a medieval settlement which lies further to its west.

Recent survey work has revealed a complex terraced garden surrounding the site of the castle, with two large fishponds occupying the valley floor immediately to its south. A revision by the author of a survey made by Exeter University students in 1976 is reproduced in figure 36. The impression gained from this survey is that Ilton Castle possessed an additional example to Keynedon Barton, of the use of ponds to front and reflect a mock-fortified house. Its location, only 5.5km to the south west of Keynedon is significant. The large terraced garden surrounding Ilton Castle is of comparable scale to that at Painsford, but is unlike the latter site in apparently being of only one period.

Dating is uncertain as very little documentary evidence survives. The only useful reference is a description of the castle when its standing remains were cleared in 1780, as a quadrangular structure with square towers at the corners (Prideaux Fox 1864, 105–6). It suggests that the castle, and by implication the garden, was abandoned by the eighteenth century. This

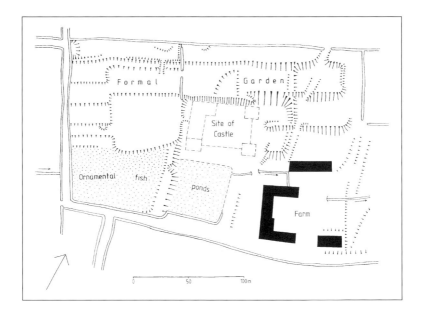

Fig. 36 Ilton Castle, Malborough. Earthworks of an extensive terraced garden surround the site of a quadrangular castle of 1337 whose battlements were reflected in two fishponds to its south, imitating a moat (© Robert Waterhouse)

should not be surprising, given the manor's distance from the main Courtenay seat at Powderham.

Langdon Court, Wembury

A courtyard mansion, largely of late seventeenth-century appearance, Langdon was owned by the Calmady family, wealthy lawyers and merchants, between 1555 and 1875. Vincent Calmady rebuilt the house in 1577 and Josias Calmady remodelled it in 1707. Brick-faced terraced gardens, probably of the late seventeenth century, lie south of the house, with pairs of contemporary gate piers fronting the south-west and south-east sides.

Lower Washbourne Barton, Ashprington

A small sixteenth to seventeenth century farmhouse with detached kitchen, the farm seems to have been bought by the Kellands of Painsford in the late seventeenth century. A part-walled garden to the north-east of the house, is in position and design identical to that at Painsford and may therefore be of late seventeenth or early eighteenth century date. Traces of a small rectangular formal garden with two terraces cut into the slope behind the house could be of similar date.

Norden, Kingsbridge

This former courtyard house of sixteenth and seventeenth century date is thought to have been used as a dower house for the large E plan Jacobean mansion of Bowringsleigh, 1km to the north west. Beyond the west end of the house and at right angles to it, a series of slight terraces are partly preserved in a nineteenth-century vegetable garden and partly in relict form in the adjoining pasture. A terraced garden, possibly of similar date to the house, seems likely. Extensive formal gardens once fronted Bowringsleigh House, but these were destroyed in the nineteenth century.

Place Barton, Higher Ashton

This large courtyard mansion was owned by the Chudleigh family from *c*.1320 – *c*.1750, although they moved their seat to nearby Haldon House in the early eighteenth century. The house developed around three south facing courtyards, with several high status buildings of fourteenth to sixteenth century date surviving. A field between the house and the church to the east contains a large terraced garden on a south facing slope, two broad flat terraces being divided by a narrow terraced walk (cf. Holcombe Court, Holcombe Rogus), which may have connected the house with the nearby church. A disturbance in the centre of each terrace scarp suggests the former positions of flights of steps. A sunken marshy area on the lowest terrace may be the site of a pond, while remains of a stone faced dam survive in the stream dividing the field from the churchyard. A long cob wall lies alongside the road to the south and may have screened the garden from the road. The terraces appear to have turned around by 90 degrees and entered the shallow valley which leads north from the house. Here, they overlooked one of two large rectangular fishponds in the valley bottom, now drained and partly filled in. Late fifteenth and early sixteenth century residential chambers in the house overlooked this area, which may have been treated as a water garden.

A small deer park of about 130 acres lay north of the house. Its irregular boundaries suggest a late, perhaps sixteenth or seventeenth-century date (Rackham 1995, 153). An estate map of 1810 (DRO, 253B/ME 1) shows elaborate tree planting schemes within this park, and an avenue leading into it from the house, which Rev. John Swete referred to in his diary entry for February 1794. He also recorded ruins of the hall in a watercolour (DRO, 564M/F5/131).

Ranscombe, Sherford

This small E plan house, possibly of 1620, has a cob walled garden in front of it, a path leading up to the entrance porch passing through this garden. During the sixteenth to early seventeenth centuries the house was owned by a minor branch of the Hals family of Keynedon (qv).

Shilston Barton, Modbury

This Domesday manor was owned by the Hill family between the fifteenth and early seventeenth centuries, followed by the Saverys who lived here until 1821. A small mansion of fifteenth to seventeenth century date stood at the head of a combe, facing south, and was recorded in an early nineteenth century watercolour now in a private collection in Australia (Modbury History Society 1980, 4). This was demolished and replaced by a triple-fronted Georgian mansion between 1811 and 1813; itself partially demolished *c.*1835. A series of four rectangular terraces of a large formal garden associated with the previous house, climb an east-facing hillside to the north. Disturbances at the sides and in the centre of each terrace scarp suggest the former position of steps between the terraces. A large early eighteenth-century walled garden lay south west of the house, while the valley below contains well-preserved remains of a rare late seventeenth and early eighteenth-century water garden (Currie, this volume). The gardens are the subject of ongoing research and survey by the present author, in advance of their restoration.

Wembury House, Wembury

The largest Elizabethan mansion in Devon, Wembury House was built by Sir John Hele, a London lawyer, in the early seventeenth century and was furnished with the astonishing number of 42 hearths, listed in the hearth tax return of 1674 (Stoate 1982, 156). No part of this mansion has survived, but a later, smaller house occupies the eastern side of a broad square court which appears to have contained an extensive formal garden. High stone walls enclose earth terraces overlooking a gently sloping central area. A raised rectangular terrace three metres high and reached by stairs, occupies the entire west side. This has remains of crenellations with carved granite merlons, and was intended to be viewed from outside as well as within. There is no parallel for this walled garden in the district.

Wembury House was completely rebuilt between 1685 and 1701, and it is this house which partially survives today. A watercolour of 1716 shows the garden viewed from the crenellated western terrace. By this time the design of the garden was restrained with occasional statues and topiary trees ornamenting a level lawn with gravel paths (Cherry 1988, 110). The house was extensively rebuilt again in the early nineteenth century. A park is recorded here, containing a salt-water fish pond on an inlet of the sea, although it is not known to what period this belonged (Polwhele 1806, 454).

References

Airs, M. 1995 *The Tudor and Jacobean Country House: A Building History*
Beacham, P. 1990 'Local Building Materials and Methods' in P. Beacham (ed.) *Devon Building*, 13–31
Blaylock, S. (forthcoming) Bowhill, Exeter
Brown, S. W. 1996 'Berry Pomeroy Castle' *Proc. Devon Archaeol. Soc.* 54, 1–335
Brown, S. W. 1999 Archaeological Survey of Berry Pomeroy Parish. Unpublished report for the Duke of Somerset
Cherry, B. 1988 'The Devon country house in the late seventeenth and early eighteenth centuries' *Proc. Devon Archaeol. Soc.* 46, 91–135
Cremers, C.M. 1973 'Our Heritage: The Dutch Garden, An Introduction to its History' *Garden History* 2, No. 1 10–29
Coope, R. 1986 'The Long Gallery: Its origins, development, use & decoration' *Architectural History* 29, 43–84
Currie, C.K. 1999 'Archaeological Excavations in the gardens of Dartington Hall, Devon, 1993–99', unpublished interim report
Emery, A. 1970 *Dartington Hall*
Everson, P. 1995 'The Gardens of Campden House, Chipping Campden, Gloucestershire' *Garden History* 17, No. 2 109–121
Fletcher, A. 1991 'An Early Ha-ha?' *Garden History* 19, No. 2 146–54

Fretwell, K. 1995 'Lodge Park, Gloucestershire: A Rare Surviving Deer Course and Bridgeman Layout' *Garden History* 23, No. 1, 133–44

Gray, T. 1995 *The Garden History of Devon*

Gray, T. (ed.) 1997 *Travels in Georgian Devon* vol. 1

Heal, V. and Waterhouse, R. (forthcoming) The Deer Park at Dartington Hall

Impey, E.A. 1999 'The Seigneurial Residence in Normandy, 1125–1225: An Anglo-Norman Tradition?' *Medieval Archaeol.* 43, 45–73

Lega-Weekes, E. 1900 'The Old Mansion of North Wyke' *Trans. Devonshire Ass.* 32, 195–205

Maxwell-Lyte, H.C. 1898 *Lists of Sheriffs for the Counties of Exeter, Devon, Cornwall, Dorset & Somerset*

Meirion-Jones, G., Jones, M. & Pilcher, J.R. 1993, 'The Seigneurial Domestic Buildings of Brittany', in G. Meirion-Jones & M. Jones (eds) Manorial domestic buildings of England and Northern France, *Society of Antiquaries Occasional Papers*, 15, 158–91

Passmore, D. 1999 'DAS Volunteers in Action' [at Shilston Barton] *Devon Archaeological Society Newsletter* 72, 4–5

Prideaux Fox, S. 1864 *Kingsbridge Estuary*

Rackham, O. 1995 *Trees and Woodland in the British Landscape*

Stoate, T.L. (ed.) 1982 *Devon Hearth Tax 1674*

Taylor, C.C, Everson, P. and Wilson-North, R. 1990 'Bodiam Castle' *Medieval Archaeol.* 34, 155–7

Various authors 1980 'Modbury: Our Inheritance' Modbury History Society, 4

Waterhouse, R. 1998 The gardens surrounding Old Forde House. Unpublished report for Teignbridge District Council

Waterhouse, R. (2000) 'Keynedon Barton, Sherford, South Devon' *Proc. Devon Archaeol. Soc.* 58, 127–200

Waterhouse, R. (forthcoming) The Medieval Manor Houses of Southern Devon, 1200–1700

Whittle, E.H. 1989 'The Renaissance Gardens of Raglan Castle' *Garden History* 17, No. 1, 83–94

Somerset Parks and Gardens, 1500–1830: Some Addenda

James Bond

Introduction

The common lament that one either publishes too soon or not at all is more than just a platitude. *Somerset Parks and Gardens* (Bond 1998) had come off the press just ten months before the Exeter conference commemorated by this volume, and it was a somewhat chastening experience to be asked at that meeting to reflect upon my sins of omission and commission quite so soon after my labours had appeared in print! However, the invitation has provided a welcome opportunity to offer some revisions and amendments and to review the subsequent progress of research.

The motivation for writing a book on the parks and gardens of Somerset arose out of personal interest following a move to the county in 1986. It was drafted in odds and ends of spare time over a period of nine years, in part building upon earlier, more limited syntheses on medieval parks (Bond 1994) and early formal gardens (Bond and Iles 1991). It was written not from a specialist background in horticulture or garden design, but rather from the standpoint of an historical geographer-turned-landscape archaeologist with wide interests in many aspects of the man-made landscape. A career spent first in the west midlands and then in the upper Thames valley had included several previous flirtations with parks and gardens, culminating in the co-editing of a study of the evolution of Blenheim Park (Bond & Tiller 1987, 1997). Somerset offered a rather different challenge. While it contained nothing on the scale of Blenheim, it did offer a quite splendid range of smaller parks and gardens with good representative examples of most periods and styles, many of which deserved to be much better known. The aim of the book was simply to offer a reasonably balanced multi-disciplinary overview of what was known of the evolution of Somerset parks and gardens over the centuries, and their impact upon the landscape. It had no axes to grind, no favourite styles of design or cultivation to promote, no ground-breaking new techniques of investigation to demonstrate, no particular conservation or management agenda.

When the book was first conceived there was still a dearth of regional or county-scale studies, one of the few exceptions being Frank Woodward's early exploration of Oxfordshire parks (Woodward 1982), which in many ways provided the first inspiration for my own work. Yet studies at this scale should open up all sorts of possibilities for exploring the varied response to local soils and climate, regional stylistic preferences, the influence of neighbours upon each other, the speed or tardiness with which metropolitan fashions reached the provinces and the extent of independent local innovation, all factors which tend to be obscured by thematic surveys or overviews at national scale. During the time that *Somerset Parks and Gardens* was in preparation, that balance began to be redressed, with surveys and gazetteers from other areas appearing in a variety of formats. Elsewhere in the South West, surveys of Cornwall were published by Helen McCabe (1988), Avon by Stewart Harding & David Lambert (1994), and Devon in a volume edited by Steven Pugsley (1994). A guide to archival, pictorial and published sources for Devon was also provided by Gray (1995). A survey of Gloucestershire was published by Mowl (2002).

No published survey of parks and gardens can ever be definitive; views prevailing at any given time will continue to be reassessed; new evidence will continue to emerge as new techniques of investigation are developed and further sources are explored; and new questions will be asked of the evidence. *Somerset Parks and Gardens* was a summary of our knowledge at a particular point in time, a step on the road towards a fuller understanding. I would have been deeply disappointed if it had marked the end of that road and had provoked no further response. Inevitably some interesting garden sites were overlooked, while the significance of others was underestimated, and I am very grateful to many friends, colleagues and correspondents who have contributed further information since that publication.

A few errors have come to light. The park at 'Knowl' listed in the 1569 musters as belonging to Sir James fitzJames was correctly identified in the list on p.54 as Knowle in Shepton Montague, but an earlier erroneous location at Knowle in Bawdrip on the first draft of Map 5.8 unfortunately survived all the way through to the published version. The reversal into mirror-image of the aerial view of Witham which appeared as fig.5.16 also escaped notice until after publication. Christopher Thacker has pointed out that, although Alfred's Tower on the Somerset portion of the Stourhead estate was designed by Flitcroft in 1762, the building was not begun until several years later, and was only completed in 1772; and in my discussion of the Royal Victoria Park at Bath I failed to make adequate reference to Frederick Hanham's 330-page manual (1857) which lists and describes its trees and shrubs (Thacker 2000).

New information has emerged on points of detail. In 1998 I was aware of only one crinkle-crankle wall in Somerset, but Richard Raynsford has informed me of the existence of another example, belonging to Westcombe House near Bruton. The house was demolished in the 1950s, but the wall, stables and two grottoes survive. The possible involvement of Humphry Repton at Marston Bigot had escaped me, until John Phibbs brought to my attention an engraving by John Peltro from a Repton illustration of 'Marston House, Wilts. [*sic*], Seat of the Earl of Cork' in William Peacock's *Polite Repository, or Pocket Companion* for February 1805 (Carter, Goode and Laurie 1982, 143; Daniels 1999, 268). Repton supplied numerous illustrations for this almanac between 1790 and 1809, mostly of places where he had been consulted in a professional capacity, though in some cases he may have paid no more than a casual visit. For urban public parks, David Lambert's survey of Weston-super-Mare has added substantially to our knowledge (Lambert 1998).

Documentary Research

The range of documentation investigated up to 1998 was, to a large extent, restricted to published secondary works, printed sources and a limited number of printed and manuscript maps. In particular the 1998 survey owed a considerable debt to the editors and compilers of the Victoria County History, and geographical imbalances in coverage to a large extent reflect the progress of their volumes. It is not the VCH's task to undertake comprehensive investigations of parks or gardens for their own sake; nevertheless, in those hundreds for which volumes do exist, any investigator is given a flying start, not just in recognising parks and gardens of particular periods, but also in the understanding of their social context and their wider impact upon the landscape.

As more family and estate papers are made more accessible through publication, further details of park and garden management are coming to light, though often the task resembles looking for needles in haystacks. For example, the correspondence of the Trevelyans of Nettlecombe, edited for publication by Mary Siraut (1990), contained an early reference to the raising of apricot trees in 1666–7 (no. 315), and some particularly informative letters sent by the agent, James Babbage, to Sir John Trevelyan, concerning the estate and garden in 1834. On Feb 11th Babbage reported that he had acquired from the nursery 200 acacias, 500 black poplars, 150 English elms and 6000 larches to be planted on different parts of the estate. Apple trees recently purchased for Colton and Court Farm had been planted and secured by stakes and 'frith'(?). The greenhouse trees and plants were looking well, and the peas and beans were growing fast since there had been no frost (no. 428). Babbage wrote again to Sir John on 22nd March reporting that 9,000 larch, 120 elm, 200 acacias and 500 black poplars had been planted at Capton Meadows at Cottiford, Beacon Hill, Pitt Wood and Huish Barton, about 500 oak, larch and spruce at Treborough, and 660 apple trees at Treborough Court Farm, Colton, Nettlecombe, Huish Barton and Slade farms, while 20,000 seedling larch had been ordered to put in the nursery at Holwell, Treborough (no. 429). On 20th October 1834 Babbage wrote again that the gardener had made about 10 gallons of wine from the grapes, that some Spanish chestnuts, which were plentifully available that year, had been gathered for Sir John's use, and that the orange trees had been moved into the greenhouse, all the external wood of which had been given a good coat of paint (no. 431). None of this is world-shaking information, but it continues to fill out the detail of how great estates were managed and the role

Fig. 37 Earthworks of garden terraces and plat at Chilcompton Manor
(© James Bond)

of parks and gardens within them. Much original archival material of this type still awaits investigation.

Earthwork Surveys

The contribution which archaeological field survey can make to garden history has been underlined by a number of recent publications (e.g. Brown 1991; Pattison 1998). The earthworks of abandoned formal gardens were first recognised on a significant scale by the Royal Commission on Historical Monuments in Cambridgeshire and Northamptonshire (Royal Commission on Historical Monuments (England) 1968, 97, 110–12, 126; 1975, 6–8, 14–16, 104–5, 113; 1979, 45–6, 72–3, 75–7, 113–15, 140–2, 148–9, 156–62; 1981, 3–4, 35–7, 40–41, 106–9, 116–19; 1982, 61–3, 84–6, 106–7, 146–8). As their characteristic features came to be defined and recognised, further examples began to come to light all over the country. In Somerset pioneer work was carried out by Mick Aston at Hardington and Low

Ham (Aston 1978). Several further sites in that part of northern Somerset which was transferred to the short-lived county of Avon in 1974 were subsequently surveyed by Rob Iles (Edgar & Iles 1981; Iles 1985; Bond & Iles 1991). Progress subsequent to that date has been slow. While a handful of further measured surveys have followed on from the discovery of previously unknown sites at Shapwick (McOmish & Brown 1993) and Over Stowey (Hollinrake and Hollinrake 1994) and, critically, the large and complex site at Low Ham has been resurveyed and reinterpreted by the Royal Commission (Wilson-North 1998), many earthwork sites still lack even the most basic of sketch surveys. The recording of all known earthwork sites should be an urgent priority, both as an aid to interpretation and as a record against any unpredictable future destruction.

Some earthworks which purport to represent other types of site may now require re-examination. For example, elsewhere in the country it has been demonstrated that many monastic sites are partly overlain by the vestiges of often short-lived post-Dissolution houses and gardens. Witham Charterhouse provides a prime local example of this (Wilson-North 1998). Similarly, some deserted medieval village sites may

Fig. 38 Earthworks of garden terraces overlooking fishpond in Henhills Copse, Shapwick (© James Bond)

incorporate remains of gardens of grander houses which succeeded them. The identification of the deserted hamlet of Nether Adber near Mudford is not in doubt but, as Rob Wilson-North has pointed out, an aerial photograph taken before the northern half of the site was partly levelled around 1970, shows there a regular circular pond and rectilinear moat-like features which are very different from the well-defined peasant house plots at the southern end (Aston 1977, Plate 2). Thomas Gerard's comment in 1633 that 'the Huntley family flourished in Nether Adber even until our grandfathers days when all of a sudden it sunk' (ed. Bates 1900, 174) seems to imply some sort of residence surviving there at least into the middle of the sixteenth century, after the village had disappeared.

Geophysical Surveys

Geophysical survey has considerable potential for garden archaeology. So far, however, its most successful application for this purpose in Somerset has been incidental to a quite different project. The Royal Commission on Historical Monuments commissioned work at Witham and Hinton Charterhouse from Geophysical Surveys of Bradford as part of a programme of archaeological survey and recording of sites of all British Carthusian monasteries. On both sites resistance readings showed up rectilinear subdivisions within the great cloister which seem unlikely to relate to any medieval use of the space. At Witham the anomalies are very probably related to the reuse of the cloister area as a garden associated with the eighteenth-century mansion of the Wyndham family (RCHME 1994). Several narrow bands of high resistance within the Hinton cloister also seem likely to be a product of former gravel paths or brick or stone drains (RCHME 1995).

It is also possible to locate pre-garden features which may have been long forgotten when the garden was laid out, or which may actually have been removed to make way for it. Geophysical survey in the gardens of West Bower Manor at Durleigh has located the footings of the circular dovecote demolished in 1967 at their southeast corner, and a demolished barn and set of animal pens immediately to the north. Further high-resistance anomalies orientated at right-

Fig. 39 Earthworks of garden terraces and plat at Parsonage Farm,
Over Stowey (© James Bond)

angles to the west wing of the present house may represent wall alignments of its fifteenth century predecessor (Jessop 1996). Elsewhere, somewhat incoherent anomalies in the central part of the garden may reflect previous phases of garden design, but here interpretation is not possible without excavation.

Case Studies

For at least half a dozen sites, a more substantial reassessment is already needed or is in hand. The first two sites (and there will undoubtedly be many more) escaped notice entirely in the 1998 survey, and still await fuller investigation. For the remainder significant advances in our understanding have already been achieved through the work of others.

Ashley Combe, Porlock

An area of elaborate nineteenth-century garden terraces set in a picturesque location amidst woods of oak, ash, beech, sweet chestnut, poplars, firs and pines, on the north Somerset coast marks the location of the now-vanished mansion of Ashley Combe. Two private roads ran through the estate parallel with the coast. The house was built in Italianate style in 1866 (Pevsner 1958, 276). In 1889 the estate was tenanted by Baroness de Taintegnie (*PSANHS* 35.i 1889, 24). The Lovelace family occupied it around the beginning of the present century. Charles Francis Annesley Voysey (1857–1941) designed a number of buildings on the estate for the Lovelaces, including a group of estate cottages dated 1936, which are amongst his last works. Lady Lovelace is said to have designed the gatehouse to Ashley Combe near Culbone church. The gardens were visited by the Somerset Archaeology and Natural History Society in 1906, though unfortunately the details recorded in their proceedings are scanty (*PSANHS* 52.i 1906, 28).

Ashwick Grove, near Shepton Mallet

Collinson (1791 ii, 449) describes the house of Ashwick Grove as newly built, 'in a very romantic situation . . . patched with immense rocks

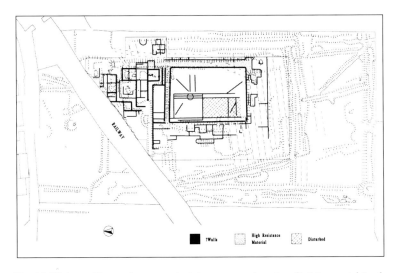

Fig. 40 Witham Charterhouse, resistivity survey showing divisions within the Carthusian Great Cloister, probably representing a formal garden attached to the eighteenth century Wyndham mansion (© GSB Prospection)

which project through the foliage from the lofty brow of the cliff'. There had been an earlier house and gardens on the site. In the early eighteenth century the dissenter Dr James Foster took refuge there, and wrote many tracts in a summerhouse. The house was occupied by the agricultural writer John Billingsley (1747–1811) and then by the Stracheys (c.1830). The house was sold for demolition in October 1955, and Robin Atthill mentions the remains of sunken gardens and winding walks leading down the valley into the woods, a broken statue of a nymph on a pedestal in a clearing, and the still-visible foundations of Foster's summerhouse (Atthill 1971, 45–6). Another garden structure, 'a simple folly, a little temple-shaped sun house carved out of rock' is mentioned by Shirley Toulson (1984, 107).

Bishop's Palace, Wells

The present appearance of the gardens of the bishop's palace at Wells still owes much to the romantic-style landscaping undertaken by Bishop Law in the 1820s (Bond 1998, 110). When describing this in 1998 I remained in blissful ignorance of the existence of John Carter's plan of c.1790 in the Society of Antiquaries' library showing many surviving elements of a more formal design. Subsequent survey and documentary work by the Archaeology Department of Bristol University has suggested that an unusually early Dutch-style garden may have been developed here in the time of Bishop Thomas Ken (1685–90), who had been chaplain to Princess Mary, wife of William of Orange, in 1679.

West Bradley

The building of the manor-house at West Bradley, attributed by Phelps (1839, i, 594) to Col. Pierce (*sic*), former lord of the manor, around 1760, had been assumed to represent the likely date of the shrubbery, plantations, lawn, fishponds and elm trees briefly described in the same source. However, I am indebted to Joan Hasler for sending me further details of

this site, including extracts from a diary compiled by John Cannon, clerk and bailiff to William Peirs (SCRO DD/SAS/c.1193/4), which show that there was an earlier, considerably more elaborate garden here. Piers was a friend of Henry Clinton, 22nd Earl of Lincoln (1684–1728), who was a member of the Kit-Kat Club, that coterie of Whig landowners, politicians and writers sharing a common interest in art, architecture and garden design; Clinton was himself developing the grounds of Oatlands near Weybridge in 1725. Cannon's diary records in 1726 that he had 'most weeks 30 employed, either in the garden or in the field, but mostly in the garden and about canals, waterworks, walks and knots under the direction of Mr Long, a Dutchman sent to him from Weybridge'. However, a quarter of a century later this was in decay. Humphrey Leicester, one of the witnesses at a Chancery case in 1750, reported that about a hundred oak, ash and elm trees had been cut down on the estate, that an avenue of young oaks planted about fourteen years previously had been taken up and removed to Peirs' new home at Baltonsborough, that Peirs had some years ago made a conduit to convey water to some meadow ground and some water-works which he had since allowed to go to ruin, and that although the house at West Bradley was in good repair, the garden was overrun with weeds (BL Add. MSS 36063).

Redlynch Park

There are records of gardens and orchards at Redlynch in the late seventeenth and early eighteenth century, but the development of a landscaped setting for the new 1708–9 mansion did not commence until Stephen Fox (later 1st Earl of Ilchester) succeeded to the estate on the death of his father in 1716. Recent work by Dr Robert Dunning (summarised in Dunning 1999, 28) has shown that this was a park of considerable significance, and an interesting example of the transition from late formality to early landscape style. An undated early eighteenth-century map shows a wide double line of trees aligned roughly north-north-west to south-south-east approaching the mansion across

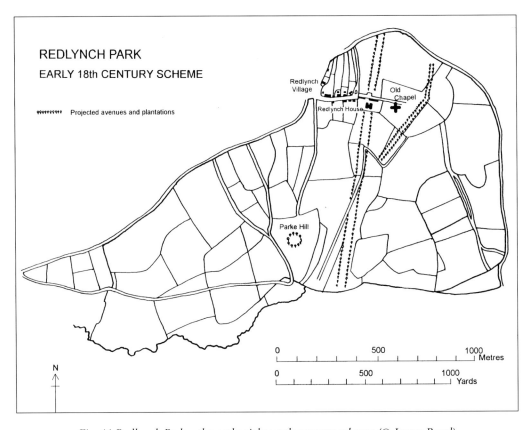

Fig. 41 Redlynch Park – the early eighteenth century scheme (© James Bond)

pasture fields from either side. To the east is shown a small plantation and a shorter avenue not aligned towards the house, and to the south-west an isolated circle of trees in a field called 'Parke Hill'. To the east of the house the map shows the chapel of Redlynch with a tower, and to the west up to a dozen cottages along either side of a short lane leading towards the mansions (DCRO, D/FSI, map). A second survey by E. Grant, dated 1738, depicts a more evolved and coherent parkland landscape covering some 520 acres. The chapel and village have now been removed from the vicinity of the house, the mansion has a new approach from the east alongside a new rectilinear plantation, and more or less parallel with this approach a grassy slope sweeps up to a terraced walk to the north. North-west of the mansion the map shows an enclosure with four terraces, perhaps serving as kitchen gardens, each containing a small tri-angular stewpond. To the west again, beyond the former village site, five short avenues con-verge upon the Dog Kennel. The northern flank of the park nearest to the mansion is closed off from the Bruton to Wincanton road by a screen of trees. All traces of the long avenue north and south of the mansion have gone, but the shorter and narrower avenue to the east re-mains. The shallow valley to the south of the mansion is shown with several discrete blocks of woodland, one containing a cruciform ar-rangement of paths converging upon a central circular glade, another containing a short length of serpentine walk leading up to the end of the older eastern avenue. There is also a large pond in full view from the house, apparently fed from a couple of balancing reservoirs concealed be-hind the woods. This is geometrically shaped, with four sides of approximately equal length, the dam following a segmental curve, the two flanking sides straight and the head with a small semicircular bay at the mid-point. Finally, 200

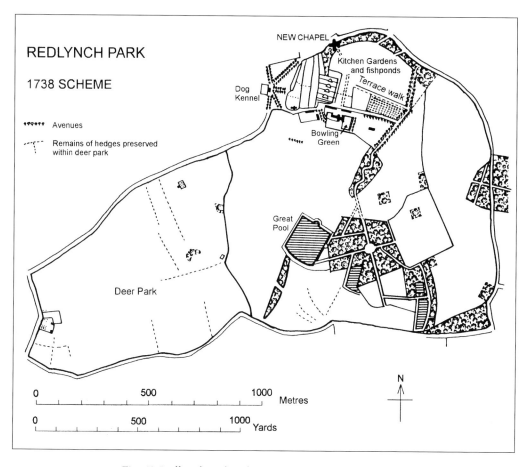

REDLYNCH PARK

1738 SCHEME

NEW CHAPEL

Kitchen Gardens and fishponds

Terrace walk

Dog Kennel

Bowling Green

Great Pool

Deer Park

♦♦♦♦♦♦ Avenues

﹣﹣﹏﹣ Remains of hedges preserved within deer park

| 0 | 500 | 1000 | Metres |

| 0 | 500 | 1000 | Yards |

N

Fig. 42 Redlynch Park – the 1738 scheme (© James Bond)

acres in the western part of the park were fenced off as a deer park, retaining many intermittent rows of trees preserved from the former hedges shown on the earlier map (Bodl. Lib. Gough maps, 29, f.21).

As always, it has to be questioned whether these maps were records of what had already been achieved, or were merely declarations of intent which might later be modified at whim. On the ground a substantial retaining wall for the northern terrace walk remains, and three of the four small fishponds can still be seen. The large geometric pond in the valley has taken on a slightly more rounded outline. Dr Dunning's examination of the Fox-Strangways papers in Dorset County Record Office has shown that some works were in hand by 1729, with brickmakers and bricklayers employed over a twelve-

year period on works which included garden walls; we hear that 'the slope and the piece of water are finished' by November 1732. The chapel was rebuilt on a new site on the northern margin of the park shortly before 1738. However, the woods seem not to have been planted before 1740, when purchase of nearly 21,000 'forest wood plants' appears in the accounts. Between 1740 and 1762 a further 230 acres were added to the south, creating a new deer park out of the fields formerly cultivated by farmers of Stony Stoke and Knowle. The 'Great Pond' was constructed in 1741 at a cost of nearly £85. A new road leading into the park from the east was commenced in 1745, and in 1750 nearly 33,000 birch, alder, thorn and holly trees were bought for planting along it. The park was walled between 1748 and 1750.

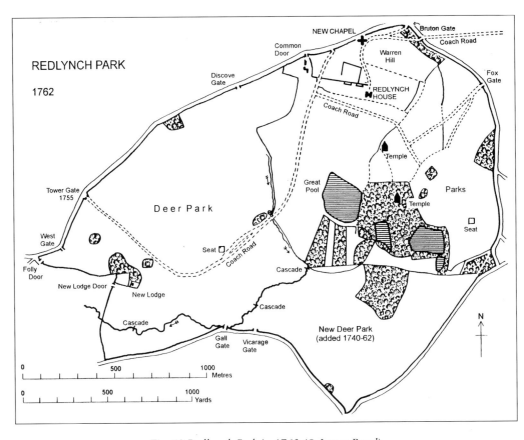

Fig. 43 Redlynch Park in 1762 (© James Bond)

In 1755 a gothick triumphal arch with heraldic shields was erected at the western entrance to the park. This was almost certainly designed by Henry Flitcroft, who was frequently at nearby Stourhead between 1744 and 1762, advising the younger Henry Hoare on the garden buildings there (in the mid-1750s Flitcroft's major project at Stourhead was the Temple of Hercules, now the Pantheon). Other features were added from time to time: a Chinese seat was added in 1756, a Temple in 1762, a Cascade in 1766. The 1738 map shows a bowling green adjoining the east side of the house, but no ornamental gardens. However, occasional references to the purchase of seeds and fruit stocks appear in the household accounts between 1738 and 1755, when John Eaton was the gardener. Seeds were purchased first from Mr Greening (presumably Thomas Greening,

the royal gardener) and then from George Newman of Sherborne. The sum of £1 16s was paid for tuberoses, jasmine and orange trees in 1743, additional orange trees were provided by Greening in 1747, and 'flowering shrubs' were delivered from Bristol in 1751. A new map of the park was made by Samuel Donne in 1762, showing it then containing over 750 acres (DCRO, D/FSI). A draft lease of 1794 lists the amenities of Redlynch as including 'walled gardens well planted with fruit trees, a hot house and greenhouse, a large menagerie, extensive pleasure grounds and woods, a large park . . . totalling 739 acres'. The particulars of 1803 add 'a beautiful shrubbery and flower garden' to the description. During the first half of the nineteenth century most of the parkland was turned over to agriculture, though a number of its ornamental features and plantations survive.

Fig. 44 Redlynch Park, the Tower Gate added at the western entrance of
the park in 1755 (© James Bond)

Mendip Lodge, Upper Langford

The existence of an important late eighteenth-century garden at Mendip Lodge, described in the correspondence of the then popular poet and novelist Anna Seward (1742–1809), was drawn to my attention in October 1999 by John Phibbs. Mendip Lodge was built by Thomas Sedgwick Whalley, son of the Regius Professor of Divinity at Cambridge, and grandson of a chancellor of Wells Cathedral who owned Winscombe Court. The letters of Anna Seward and of Thomas Sedgwick Whalley have been published (Scott 1810; Constable 1811; Wickham 1863), but copies are rare, and at the time of writing I have been unable to gain access to the volumes of Whalley's correspondence. The most relevant parts of Anna Seward's papers are included as an appendix to this article. The following summary is based partly upon a valuable but previously-overlooked account of Whalley's career and details of his house and grounds by Vincent Waite (1954, 129–33), amplified by further documentary and archaeological survey undertaken by Kate Addison (2000). Whalley was a poet and noted spendthrift, who spent much of his youth touring the continent. Each of his three marriages seems to have been motivated primarily by the need to salvage his finances; on two occasions the

ploy was successful, on the third occasion not. His first marriage was to a wealthy widow some years his senior, who was heiress to Langford Court. After ten years of heavy expenditure he was forced to lease out Langford Court and built a smaller house nearby. He chose a wooded site on the northern flank of Mendip, commanding wide views over the Vale of Wrington, where he was soon entertaining a wide circle of friends, including the actress Sarah Siddons, the educational philanthropist Hannah More, the writer Hester Lynch Piozzi and the anti-slavery campaigner William Wilberforce. Mendip Lodge was designed as a summer residence, being closed up when the Whalleys retired to their town house at the Royal Cresent in Bath.

The grounds laid out at Mendip Lodge were praised by one visitor in the late eighteenth century, who admired 'the loveliest architectural luxury I ever saw . . . It hangs over the traveller at a considerable distance, and at first sight appears inaccessible; but the ascent is so gradual and easy that we are soon surprised to find ourselves on an Italian verandah 84ft long, looking down on innumerable towers, steeples and villages. In every direction are steep and verdant walks, and the grounds contain 52 grottoes, one for every week in the year'.

Another visitor, the essayist and critic Thomas de Quincy, was more scathing: '. . . a show place in which a vast deal of money had been sunk upon two follies, equally unproductive of pleasure to the beholder and of anything approaching a pecuniary compensation to the owner . . . Out of doors there are terraces of a mile long, one rising above another and carried by mere artifice of mechanical skill along the perpendicular face of a lofty rock. Had they when finished any particular beauty? Not at all. Considered as a pleasure-ground they formed a far less delightful landscape and a far less alluring haunt than most of the uncostly shrubberies which were seen below in unpretending situations and upon the ordinary level of the Vale! What a record of imbecility! . . . No part of the grounds, nor the house itself, was at all the better because originally it has been beyond measure difficult to build it'.

Both accounts contain elements of exagger-

ation. Stories of fifty-two grottoes and mile-long terraces take some swallowing. However, the grounds were clearly striking enough to provoke strong reactions. Sadly, Whalley was not to enjoy his creation for many more years. After the death of his first wife in 1801 he married a wealthy lady from Wiltshire and proceeded to squander her fortune, continuing to occupy Mendip Lodge during the summer months and taking up winter quarters in Bath. His second wife died in 1805, and in 1813 he married a widow from Bath who turned out to be far less wealthy than he had been led to believe; and since she, too, had been under the delusion that he was well-heeled, they were both disappointed and soon went their separate ways. Mendip Lodge was put up for sale at £30,000, but remained unsold for twenty years, and Whalley died in exile in France in 1828 in 'a common lodging-house' at the age of 82.

Sales particulars of 1844 and 1903 (SCRO:

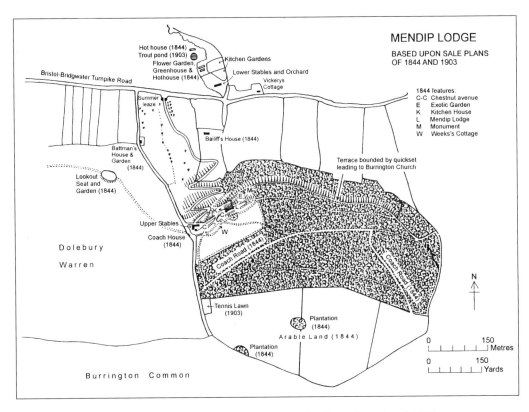

Fig. 45 Mendip Lodge, plan based upon sale plans of 1844 and 1903
(© James Bond)

DD/X/MT 5, DD/OB 15) provide further details of the layout, which have been discussed by Addison (2000). The 1844 catalogue describes the main house as being on a hill slope surrounded by plantations, with walks and drives on the greensward, a plateau and a terrace about half a mile long leading to Burrington church. It also describes plantations, shrubberies, large walled gardens, hothouses and greenhouses. A spring was conducted into a cold bath, with a nearby building used as a dressing-room. There were two circular entrance lodges at the start of the half-mile-long road through the gardens, and stables for eighteen horses. The accompanying map shows the house approached by a winding road leading up to a chestnut avenue, with gardens terminating in a quickset hedge along the walk to Burrington church, a circular plantation in the woods, a lookout seat with its own garden, and a small area of flower gardens, with a fishpond and hothouse beyond the new turnpike road to the north.

The lodge is shown in an engraving from a watercolour published by Rutter (1829, 112). The whole front of the house was spanned by a two-decker verandah with an informal terrace overlooking a sloping lawn with mixed planting of conifers and deciduous trees around.

Mendip Lodge enjoyed a brief revival in the second half of the nineteenth century, when the Somers family restored the house, gardens and walks to their original beauty, but this could not be sustained, and in 1903 the house was offered for sale again. The 1903 sale catalogue emphasizes the beauty of the views over the Bristol Channel towards Wales, and the value of the pheasant and rabbit shooting. A golf course had recently been laid out on part of the warren. Giant beech, oak, elm, chestnut, ash, fir and pine woods adorned the grounds. The terraces above the house included a bowling-green, tennis courts and a lawn with a tea-house. Near the park gates were two walled kitchen gardens, a small flower garden and orchard, with glasshouses, a vinery with 15 vines and a gardener's cottage. One feature recorded in 1844 which finds no mention in 1903 is the spring-fed cold bath, and this may by then have disappeared. The circular plantation in the

woods has also become overgrown and lost.

By the 1930s the lodge had ceased to be used as a residence, the buildings fell into ruin and the pleasure-grounds were finally abandoned. In 1954 Vincent Waite vividly described the decaying ruins, the paths strangled by weeds and overhanging bushes, and a wilderness of brambles covering the slopes which were once smooth lawns. The façade and verandah escaped the demolition of the rest of the house in the mid-1950s, surviving to be photographed in 1967, and some ruins of the front wall with its gothick windows remain today. Kate Addison's survey located a number of surviving features in the grounds, including the zigzag approach drive, remains of pathways, steps, banks and terraces with revetments, some surviving trees from the chestnut avenue, the platform of the bowling green, ruins of the upper stables and of a couple of the estate cottages, and fragments of the lookout and several further grottoes (Addison 2000).

Appendix

Descriptions of Mendip Lodge by Anna Seward

(1) Fifteen stanzas were addressed to the Rev. Thomas Sedgwick Whalley, on leaving his seat, Mendip Lodge, in Somersetshire, October 10th 1804, of which the following provide a sample (ed. Scott 1810, iii, 362–5):

High on thy mountain eminence I stand
Or range the lawny walk, that zones its
    brow,
See vales, and woods, and lesser hills
    expand,
As in a map, the verdant slopes below.

Pledges of life, see villas throng'd acquire
Sweet power to socialize the blooming
    plains:
Pledges of Life Eternal, many a spire
Turn to the orient sun their golden vanes

*While yonder, stretching far its amber
    line,*
*Dividing England from the Cambrian
    strand,*
*Wide in the blush of morning glows the
    brine*
*That bears our commerce to each distant
    land.*

*There, seen from the full shades that
    crown thy hill,*
Or from thy Gay Veranda's light arcade,
*With poignant transport does the bosom
    fill,*
If peace and joy its secret sense pervade.

(2) Extract from a letter from Anna Seward to
Lady Gresley from Langford Cottage, July 30th,
1791 (ed. Constable 1811, iii, 96–101):

At ten o'clock Mr Whalley arrived in his
chaise to conduit me to his Eden, among
the Mendip mountains. Singularly, and
beyond my high-raised expectations,
beautiful did I indeed find it: situated,
built, furnished, and adorned in the very
spirit of poetic enthusiasm, and polished
simplicity. It is about twelve years since
Mr Whalley began to cover, with a pro-
fusion of trees and shrubs, one of these
vast hills, then barren like its brethren.
The plantations seem already to have
attained their full size, strength and
exuberance of foliage.

By the addition of another horse, to help
the chaise-horses, we ascended the sylvan
steep. At about two-thirds of its height,
on a narrow terrace, stands the dear white
cottage, whose polished graces seem smil-
ingly to deride its name, though breathing
nothing heterogeneous to cottage simplicity. [A description of the house and its
internal arrangement follows] . . . the
offices at a little distance, detached from
the house, many steps below this bank,
and screened from sight by trees . . . My
apartment . . . is behind the boudoir [on
the second floor], its window at the end
of the house, looking to the east, and upon

a steep lawn, sprinkled over with larches,
poplars and woodbines, excluded, by a
circular plantation from all prospect of
that magnificent vale, upon which the
front rooms look down, in constant and
almost perpendicular descent. A gravel-
walk winds up this secluded lawn to the
mountain top . . . The wide extended vale
beneath us has every possible scenic
beauty, excepting only the meanders of a
river. Scarce two hundred yards from the
villa, on the left hand, a bare brown
mountain intersects this its woody neighbour, and towers equal heights. The protection it extends from the north-west
winds has been every thing to Mr Whalley,
as to the growth and health of his plantations. Sloping its giant's foot to the valley,
it finely contrasts, with barren sterility, the
rich cultivation of the scenery below, and
the lavish umbrage that curtains these
slopes.

With the sort of sensation that a beauteous
country girl, in the first glow of youth
and health, surveys an antiquated dow-
ager of rank and riches, seems this little
villa to look down on the large stone mansion of Langford Court, the property of
Mr and Mrs Whalley, and their former
residence. It stands in the valley, about
half a mile from us, encircled by its fine
lawn of two hundred acres, planted and
adorned with great taste. Yet more immediately below us nestles, in a wood, the
village of Langford. The smoke of its
farms and cottages, curling amongst the
trees at early morn, imparts the glow of
vitality and cheerfulness to our romantic
retirement. I climb, by seven o'clock in a
morning, the highest terrace, and "drink
the spirit of a mountain gale", which
seems to invigorate my whole frame, and
give my lungs the freest respiration. Never
more did I breathe, for any continuance,
an atmosphere so sublimated. The extensive vale finely breaks into irregulari-
ties by knolls and dingles. The beautiful
fields wearing, from the late rains, the
brightest verdure, have waved outlines of

plenteous hedge-moss, and appear, by their depth from the eye, shining and smooth as the lawns of our nobility. They are interspersed with thick and dark, though not large, woods. The whole wide expanse is dotted over by white rough-cast cottages, and here and there a village spire and squiral chateau.

Fifteen miles in width, and about seven distant from this elevation, the Bristol Channel lies, a sheet of silver, stretched longitudinally over the vale. Beyond we plainly discern the Welsh coast, whose mountains bound the horizon.

Mr Whalley's walks and bowers are finely diversified, "Shade over shade, a woody theatre".

The several terraces ascending over each other are connected by steep winding paths for the active, and by grassy steps for the feeble. These terraces are so variously planted and disposed, as to avoid all that sameness to which, from their situation, they were liable: now secluded and gloomy, now admitting the rich world below to burst upon the eye. Hermitages and caves, cut into the rocky steeps, contain rustic seats, dedicated to favourite friends, by poetic inscriptions – One to Mrs Siddons; another to Miss Hannah More; another to the accomplished Mr Jackson of Bath; one to Mr Whalley's venerable mother; another to Mr Inman, the excellent clergyman of this parish; one to Sophie Weston; and one to myself. These grottoes relieve us perpetually by their seats amidst ascents so nearly perpendicular.

On the summit of this pendant garden we find a concave lawn, with a large root-house in the centre of that semicircular bank, whose thick curtains of firs, larches, poplars &c form a darkly verdant fringe, that, rising above the root-house, crowns the mountain-top. This rustic pavilion, supported by pillars made of the boles of old trees, and twined round by woodbines and sweetpeas, is open in front, and commands the whole splendour of the vale below. It contains a large table, on which we lay our work, our writing, or our book, which we carry thither in a morning, whenever the weather will permit. Hitherto the skies have not shone upon us with much summer warmth and brightness . . .

(3) Extract from a letter from Anna Seward to Mrs Mompesson, August 23rd, 1791 (ed. Constable 1811, iii, 103)

I acknowledge the kindness of your last letter, my dear Mrs M., in the sweet retreat of my friend, Mr Whalley: from the paradise he has opened in the wild bosom of one of the vast Mendip mountains. They extend twenty miles in a chain, fronting the Bristol Channel, and there I am, beneath the roof of his cottage, which, in its white frock of rough-cast, clings near the summit of the steep ascent, with all its pines and laurels waving about it. Never was there a retirement at once so total and gay; – total from its umbrageous seclusion – gay from the gorgeous vale it commands, over which the sea stretches one of her wide arms, and over whose intervening surface are spread, in luxurious expanse, "Hill, dale, and shady wood, and sunny plain" . . .

(4) Extract from a letter from Anna Seward, now returned to Lichfield, to Mrs Stokes, December 10th 1791 (ed. Constable 1811, iii, 107):

A late letter from Mr Whalley contains a delightful winter's landscape of his view from the lofty and rocky eminence on which stands his pine-sheltered villa. I cannot resist the temptation of transmitting it here:

"Our beloved cottage still has charms for us. Use cannot pall, nor custom stale, its infinite variety. Elevated as we are, the south-west hurricanes pass innoxious over our heads, because we have plantations of evergreens, as you know, and terraces that rise above us to nearly the mountain's summit; and because the more lofty mountain, which intersects us on the left, forms our sheltering screen. But those hurricanes rush with tenfold violence through the vale beneath us, while our comforts within are undamped by the rain and unchilled by the frosts. A thousand cottages, undescried in the leafy summer, now shew their white cheerful faces. The brook, which you called a *nothing*, and which, during the softer seasons, is, in truth, most shallow and simple, now runs expanded, and foams with turbulent pride at our feet; while the more distant moors, covered with water, perfectly resemble a majestic river, rolling between us and the sea". Is this not a salvatorial sketch?

Acknowledgements

I am grateful for their assistance to the staffs of the English Faculty Library of Oxford University and of the County Record Offices of Dorset and Somerset. The following have kindly notified me of corrections and sent me additions to my 1998 text: Joan Hasler gave me some valuable material on West Bradley; Carol Hudson's enquiry alerted me to the misidentification of Knowle in Shepton Montague with Knowle in Bawdrip on my map 5.8; Naomi Payne first made me aware of John Carter's plan and the evidence for an earlier formal layout at the Bishop's Palace at Wells; John Phibbs drew my attention to Mendip Lodge and to the correspondence of Anna Seward, and also to the possible involvement of Repton at Marston Bigot; Penny Stokes informed me of the potential interest of Ashwick Grove; Richard Raynsford notified me of the Westcombe House crinkle-crankle; I owe the information on Peirs's friendship with Henry Clinton, Earl of Lincoln, to John Winstone. My attention was drawn to Ashley Combe independently by both Chris Wiltshire and Rob Wilson-North. I owe apologies to Mick Aston for the unnoticed inversion of his aerial view of Witham Charterhouse. I would like to acknowledge especially the assistance of Dr Robert Dunning, who very kindly loaned me his notes on Redlynch and permitted me advance use of information from the Bruton Hundred volume of the Victoria History of Somerset (which has since appeared in print); and to Kate Addison for permitting me to use material from her MA Landscape Archaeology dissertation submitted to the University of Bristol in September 2000.

References

Addison, K. 2000 *A Dissertation on the Garden History of Mendip Lodge Estate, North Somerset* (unpublished MA dissertation, Dept. of Archaeology, University of Bristol)

Aston, M.A. 1977 'Deserted settlements in Mudford parish, Yeovil' *Somerset Archaeol. Natur. Hist.* 121, 41–53

Aston, M.A. 1978 'Gardens and earthworks at Hardington and Low Ham, Somerset.' *Somerset Archaeol. Natur. Hist.* 122, 12–17

Atthill, R. 1971 *Old Mendip* (second edition)

Bates, E.H. (ed.) 1900 *The Particular Description of the County of Somerset drawn up by Thomas Gerard of Trent, 1633* (Somerset Record Soc. 15)

Bodl. Lib.: Bodleian Library, Oxford

Bond, C.J. 1994 'Forests, chases, warrens and parks in medieval Wessex' in Aston, M. & Lewis, C. (eds) *The Medieval Landscape of Wessex* (Oxbow Monograph 46), 115–58

Bond, C.J. 1998 *Somerset Parks and Gardens: a Landscape History*

Bond, C.J. & Iles, R. 1991 'Early gardens in Somerset and Avon', in Brown (ed.) 1991, 35–52

Bond, C.J. & Tiller, K. (eds) 1987, revised edn 1997 *Blenheim: Landscape for a Palace*

Brown, A.E. (ed.) 1991 *Garden Archaeology* (Council for British Archaeology Research Report 78)

Carter, G., Goode, P., & Laurie K. 1982 *Humphry Repton, Landscape Gardener, 1752–1818*

Collinson, J. 1791 *The History and Antiquities of the County of Somerset* (3 vols)

Constable, A. (ed.) 1811 *Letters of Anna Seward, written between the years 1784 and 1807* (6 vols)

DCRO Dorset County Record Office

Daniels, S. 1999 *Humphry Repton: Landscape*

Gardening and the Geography of Georgian England

Dunning, R.W. (ed.) 1999 *The Victoria History of the Counties of England: A History of the County of Somerset, 7: Bruton, Horethorne and Norton Ferris Hundreds (Wincanton and neighbouring parishes)*

Edgar, J. & Iles, R. 1981 'Kelston village, manor house and garden remains' *Bristol Archaeological Research Group Review* 2, 66–72

Gray, T. 1995 *The Garden History of Devon: an Illustrated Guide to Sources*

Hanham, F. 1857 *A Manual for the Park* [Royal Victoria Park, Bath]

Harding, S. & Lambert, D. 1994 *Parks and Gardens of Avon*

Hollinrake, C. & Hollinrake, N. 1994 *Parsonage Farm, Over Stowey: Archaeological Landscape Survey* (unpub. report, privately circulated)

Iles, R. 1985 'Claverton manor-house and garden', in Iles, R. & White, H. (eds) 'Avon Archaeology, 1984' *Bristol and Avon Archaeology* 5, 61–2

Jessop, O. 1996 'A recent geophysical survey of the gardens of West Bower Manor, Durleigh' *Somerset Archaeol. Natur. Hist.* 140, 53–60

Lambert, D. 1998 *Historic Public Parks: Weston-super-Mare*

McCabe, H. 1988 *Houses and Gardens of Cornwall: a Personal Choice*

McOmish, D. & Brown, G. 1993 'Earthwork surveys at Shapwick', in Aston, M.A. & Costen, M.D. (eds) *The Shapwick Report: a Topographical and Historical Study* 4, 43–4

Mowl, T. 2002 *Historic Gardens of Gloucestershire*

Pattison, P. (ed.) 1998 *There by Design: Field Archaeology in Parks and Gardens* British Archaeological Reports, British Series 26

Pevsner, N. 1958 *The Buildings of England: South and West Somerset*

Phelps, W. 1836 *The History and Antiquities of Somersetshire*

PSANHS Proceedings of the Somerset Archaeological and Natural History Society

Pugsley, S. (ed.) 1994 *Devon Gardens: an Historical Survey*

Royal Commission on Historical Monuments (England) 1968, *An Inventory of Historical Monuments in the County of Cambridge, 1: West Cambridgeshire*

Royal Commission on Historical Monuments (England) 1975 *An Inventory of the Historical Monuments in the County of Northampton, 1: Archaeological Sites in North-East Northamptonshire*

Royal Commission on Historical Monuments (England) 1979 *An Inventory of the Historical Monuments in the County of Northampton, 2: Archaeological Sites in Central Northamptonshire*

Royal Commission on Historical Monuments (England) 1981 *An Inventory of the Historical Monuments in the County of Northampton, 3: Archaeological Sites in North-West Northamptonshire*

Royal Commission on Historical Monuments (England) 1982 *An Inventory of the Historical Monuments in the County of Northampton, 4: Archaeological Sites in South-West Northamptonshire*

Royal Commission on the Historical Monuments of England 1994 *Report on Geophysical Survey: Witham Carthusian Monastery* (Royal Commission on the Historical Monuments of England, Report 94 / 21)

Royal Commission on the Historical Monuments of England 1995 *Report on Geophysical Survey: Hinton Charterhouse* (Royal Commission on the Historical Monuments of England, Report 95 / 49)

Rutter, J. 1829 *Delineations of the North Western Division of Somersetshire*

SCRO Somerset County Record Office

Scott, W. (ed.) 1810 *The Poetical Works of Anna Seward, with Extracts from her Literary Correspondence* (3 vols)

Siraut, M. (ed.) 1990 *The Trevelyan Letters to 1840* (Somerset Record Soc. 80)

Thacker, C. 2000 Review of Bond, C.J. 1998, *Somerset Parks and Gardens*, in *Trans. Ancient Monuments Soc.* 44, 156–7

Toulson, S. 1984 *The Mendip Hills: a Threatened Landscape*

Waite, V. 1954 'The northern fringe' in Coysh, A.W., Mason, E.J. & Waite, V. *The Mendips*, 123–54

Wickham, H. (ed.) 1863 *Journals and Correspondence of Thomas Sedgwick Whalley, D.D., of Mendip Lodge, Somerset* (2 vols)

Wilson-North, R. 1998 'Two relict gardens in Somerset: their changing fortunes through the 17th and 18th centuries, as revealed by field evidence and other sources' in Pattison, P. (ed.) 1998, 56–64

Woodward, F. 1982 *Oxfordshire Parks*

From Pillow Mounds to Parterres: A Revelation at Cerne Abbas

Hazel Riley and Robert Wilson-North

This article was originally published in a volume entitled
Patterns of the Past *(Pattison et al (eds) 1999).*

Introduction

In the 1950s the Royal Commission on the Historical Monuments of England surveyed and described an area of earthworks to the north-east of the site of the Benedictine Abbey of Cerne Abbas. The description concludes as follows: "The purpose of these mounds and enclosures has not been explained" (RCHME 1952, 79–80). In 1977 the Ordnance Survey Archaeology Division classified the earthworks as probable post-Dissolution pillow mounds and in 1991 one of the authors visited the site and recognised the earthworks as ornamental (NMR no ST 60 SE 41).

The development of garden archaeology as a discipline over the past two decades has meant that these earthworks can be interpreted as the remains of formal gardens. Moreover, research by various fieldworkers has enabled these garden remains to be placed within a framework recognising that many monastic sites contain elaborate, post-Dissolution garden remains, associated with the country houses which re-used these sites (Everson *et al* 1991, 47; Taylor 1991, 2).

The present survey of the earthworks at Cerne Abbas adds little extra detail to the plan published in *Dorset I* (RCHME 1952, 78). However, the perceptions which arise from a large-scale survey, reflect the use of archaeological field survey as a tool for understanding the landscape: not simply plan making.

The town of Cerne Abbas (Fig. 48) is located within the valley of the River Cerne, at its junction with two dry tributary valleys occupying an important communication route at a river crossing. The town lies on an open area at the confluence of these valleys which allowed the settlement to develop in the medieval period. Prehistoric and Romano-British activity is evident on the surrounding chalk downland in the form of settlements and field systems, such as those on Giant Hill, Black Hill and Smacam Down. The Cerne Abbas Giant, a chalk-cut hill figure of alleged Roman date, overlooks the town and still dominates the landscape.

Cerne Abbas

The Abbey

The first clear reference to the Abbey at Cerne Abbas is from the late tenth century, although there may have been a small monastery at the site before this (VCH 1908, 54). Ailmer, the Duke of Cornwall, gave the relics of Edwold to the church of Cerne, and built or rebuilt the monastery, which was dedicated to St Peter. This was completed in the year 967. After the death of his wife, Ailmer wanted the monks to observe the rule of St Benedict (Leland, quoted in VCH 1908, 54). The foundation charter for that year grants the monks at Cerne land and property in the surrounding area (VCH 1908, 54); the Domesday Survey gives the total land of the church of St Peter as 113 hides and 3 virgates, valued at £115 (VCH 1968, 74–7). An assess-

ment of the income of the abbey in 1291 was £177 8s; in 1535 it was £575 17s 4d (VCH 1908, 54).

The site of the Abbey of Cerne lies on the northern edge of the town. The Abbey Precinct occupied a roughly rectangular block, defined on the west by the River Cerne, on the east by Giant Hill and on the south by the town itself: its limits have been perpetuated by both earthworks and present day field boundaries. Within the Precinct, the site of the Abbey is now marked by several medieval buildings and an area of earthworks. Abbey Farm and its associated outbuildings and gardens occupies the western half, whilst the earthworks lie to the east. The Precinct was approached from Abbey Street which formed the principal axis of the town and led directly to the former Abbey Gatehouse.

Five medieval buildings associated with the Abbey of Cerne survive. They are the Tithe

Fig. 46 Air photograph of Cerne Abbas, showing the chalk figure – The Giant – and the garden earthworks beyond (© Crown copyright. NMR)

Barn, lying on the southern edge of the town at Barton Farm, and four buildings which all lie within the area of the former Precinct: the porch of the Abbot's Hall, the "Guest House", the Barn and a fragment of the Abbey Gatehouse, now incorporated into Abbey Farm (RCHME 1952, 77–9).

The porch of the Abbot's Hall, now standing alone, is the most impressive structure. It was built at the end of the fifteenth century, and consists of a three storey block containing a vaulted entrance passage with porter's accommodation to the north. The former Abbot's Hall lay to the east and is no longer visible except for wall scars on the east wall of the porch. The "Guest House", also of fifteenth century date, consists of a two storey range. Several alterations, all roughly contemporary, suggest that the building underwent a change of use sometime in the fifteenth century. The barn, probably also built in the fifteenth century, has been extensively altered. There are no traces of the conventual buildings; these presumably lay to the east of both Abbey Farm and the porch of the Abbot's Hall (RCHME 1952, 77), in an area subsequently occupied by the post-Dissolution residence and its formal gardens.

Fig. 47 Cerne Abbey and formal garden earthworks (drawn by Deborah Cunliffe) (© Crown copyright. NMR)

The Development of the Town

The earlier core of the settlement at Cerne Abbas is to the west of the River Cerne. Here a linear straggle of houses and narrow properties lies along Acreman Street. South of this is the fourteenth century tithe barn at Barton Farm, where settlement earthworks were recorded in 1952 (RCHME 1952, 84–5).

The main part of the settlement at Cerne Abbas, centred on Long Street, is a planned town, shaped by the existence of the monastery. The history of the Abbey has been recorded elsewhere in some detail (VCH 1908, 53–7). There are many instances of grants of lands and rents to the Abbey from both Cerne and surrounding villages. For example, in 1318 Edward II granted a licence for the monks to acquire lands and rents to the yearly value of £10. They obtained 5 messuages, 30 acres of land and a moiety of

an acre of meadow in Cerne, a further 5 messuages and land in Cerne and Middlemarsh and 10 acres of land in Wootton by Bridport (VCH 1908, 55). Particularly pertinent is the undated charter from Henry II to the monks of Cerne, which included the right of "forum" (market) in the vill of Cerne (VCH 1908, 55).

The core of the medieval town, which lies on the south side of the Abbey Precinct, is a "T"-shaped arrangement formed by Long Street, running west-east, and Abbey Street, running northwards from it. Narrow properties stretch back from the street frontages forming a compact block. Abbey Street, which contains some early sixteenth century buildings, is aligned on the Abbey Gatehouse, and shows that the town was a planned adjunct of the monastery. The junction of the "T" originally formed the market place, where, to the west and east, Long Street widens to accommodate

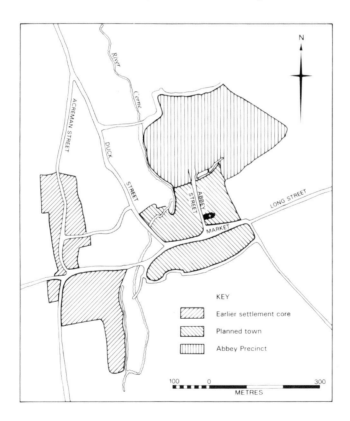

Fig. 48 Cerne Abbas: the development of the town (drawn by Deborah Cunliffe) (© Crown copyright. NMR)

it. Part of the market is clearly visible to the east of the junction, where an island of later buildings now occupy its site.

The parish church of St Mary lies a little way up Abbey Street, and appears to have been inserted into the settlement plan, explained by its early fourteenth century foundation date. The graveyard, which contains a fifteenth century churchyard cross and table-top tombs dating to the seventeenth and eighteenth centuries, is separated from the church, being at the top of Abbey Street, close to Abbey Farm. If this perpetuates the site of the Abbey graveyard, then it may be continuing a long tradition; alternatively, pressures of space in the busy market place may have led to the development of a new burial area away from the crowded town centre. The graveyard contains St Augustine's Well, partly enclosed by rubble walls of medieval date, and allegedly close to the site of the Abbey Church; a Purbeck marble effigy of an Abbot, dating from the early thirteenth century was found around here, as were portions of tile pavements (RCHME 1952, 77). The well feeds two ponds, which may be the remains of fish ponds, perhaps originally associated with the Abbey, but which clearly played a part in the post-Dissolution landscaping.

The post-Dissolution House and Formal Gardens

On March the 15th 1539 the Abbot, prior and 15 monks surrendered the Abbey to the king (VCH 1908, 57). The monastery and demesne land was let to Phillip Vanwilder, who in turn leased the main gatehouse to one Henry Williams, who lived there for some 20 years (Gibbons 1962, 50). In the early seventeenth century Sir Thomas Freke of Shroton bought the manor and farm (Hutchins 1870, 17). The Frekes were originally farmers, who came to Shroton (also called Iwerne Courtney) in the late fifteenth century. Robert Freke, a prominent person in the county of Dorset, was Auditor and Teller of the Exchequer during the reigns of Henry VIII and Elizabeth I. He was responsible for increasing his estates; when he died in

1592 he was reputed to be worth more than £100,000. Robert's son, Thomas, born in 1563, became a Member of Parliament for Dorset, and continued to increase the family estates. Sir Thomas Freke paid for the rebuilding of the nave, north aisle and south chapel of Iwerne Courtney church in 1610 (Taylor 1970, 145), perhaps around the same time as his purchase of the manor of Cerne Abbas. The manor passed to Freke's descendants, then to the Pitts of Stratfield Say; in 1870 it was owned by Lord Rivers (Hutchins 1870, 17). The estate was sold in 1919 and again in 1937 (DRO: D795/7; D/COO/J/48–51; D351/1) and it remains in private hands to the present day.

During the Freke's tenure, Denzil, Lord Holles, a distinguished Royalist, married the widow of John Frekes and lived at Cerne. Hutchins writes that Lord Holles was responsible for repairing and enlarging the "mansion house situated at the north or higher end of the market street, which seems to have been mostly built out of the ruins of the abbey" (1870, 27). He also records that "The old abbey house, many large barns, dog kennels, made out of the ruins of the abbey, were burnt, about 1740, with the dogs and horses" (Hutchins 1870, 28).

Although no contemporary description or depiction of this building survives, it clearly lay on the roughly level area immediately east of the porch of the Abbot's Hall. The field to the north was called House Close in the nineteenth century (DRO: DCO T/CEA). The house presumably incorporated elements of the conventual buildings and the survival of several monastic structures suggests that a wholesale programme of demolition and rebuilding was not undertaken.

The approach to the house is also unknown, but it is most likely to have perpetuated the monastic arrangement via the gatehouse from Abbey Street. No doubt the approach was enhanced by the ponds to the east; Abbey Street may once have bridged these to arrive at the former gatehouse. The effect thus created was one of transition from the main street of the town, across water and through the former gatehouse and Precinct walls, into the environs of the great house.

The gardens lay on the eastern and north-eastern sides of the house and are now marked by a series of well defined earthworks which form the core of the earthwork survey. To the south is the parish graveyard and St Augustine's Well. To the north of the site of the house is a square sunken area which may be a former pond or other ornamental feature. The bulk of the earthworks lie eastwards from the site of the house, separated from it by a massive north-south scarp, and stretch as far as Giant Hill. Access from the house was by a gap in the terrace scarp to the west of the cascade. The gardens form a wedge-shaped arrangement defined by a broad flat-topped bank with external ditch on the south-east and south. This feature not only defines the extent of the gardens, but also functioned as a raised walk and canal. It probably also perpetuates the line of the Abbey Precinct boundary.

Water clearly played an important part in the appearance of the gardens. Their north-eastern and southern sides were defined by canals, and the main approach to the house arrived across a chain of ponds emanating from St Augustine's Well. Another pond exists in the garden of Abbey Farm. Within the main garden are a number of water features. The three circular mounds with encircling ditches were part of a water parterre. The massive, quarry-like feature functioned as a cascade supplied from the canal to the north-west. Its present amorphous shape is due to stone-robbing.

The house would have commanded a view over the churchyard and village. The surrounding landscape combined the formal gardens with elements of the picturesque: the Abbot's Hall and Abbey Guesthouse, with the church tower and thatched cottages of the village beyond. The Cerne Abbas Giant and the Trendle, on the hillside to the north, must also have been important landscape features at this time. This aspect of its situation has been preserved in the field name, Beaver or Beauvoir (DRO: DCO D/PIT/P5; Hutchins 1870, 28). Indeed, Hutchins recognised this as a garden: "East of the present house, under the south point of the hill, are traces of a garden with walks and round parterres, which goes by the name of Beauvoir"

(1870, 28). As well as the earthworks, the landscape still contains some seventeenth century elements. Close to St Augustine's Well are the supports for a table or bench which date to the seventeenth or eighteenth century and suggest that the well may have functioned as a grotto at this time; the gateway to the churchyard is of seventeenth century date (RCHME 1952, 77).

It would seem most likely on typological grounds that these formal gardens, with their extensive use of water features, date from the early part of the seventeenth century. A beautifully drawn estate map of 1768 (DRO: DCO D/PIT P5) shows the garden remains as earthworks by this time. The documentary evidence for the immediate post-Dissolution period is scarce, but either of the two seventeenth century owners could have planned the new house and gardens. The most likely candidate would seem to be Sir Thomas Freke, a man of notable wealth as shown by his generosity to the parishoners of Iwerne Courtney. Indeed, in the parish church of Cerne, a flurry of additions and alterations occurred in the 1630s, with a new altar, a new east window (probably taken from the abbey ruins) and a new pulpit. Perhaps Sir Thomas was investing a little in the church, after such an outlay of capital as a new house and gardens.

Acknowledgements

The authors would like to thank the Lord Digby, for allowing access to the site, the staff at the Dorset Record Office, Dorchester, for their assistance, and Deborah Cunliffe and Philip Newman, who prepared the illustrations for publication. Thanks are also due to Oxbow Books for allowing this version of the original article to be reproduced.

References

Dorset Record Office, Dorchester (DRO), DCO D795/7; D/COO/J/48–51; D351/1: Sale Particulars of Cerne Abbey Estate, DCO T/

CEA: Tithe Map of Cerne Abbas, 1844, DCO D/PIT P5: Cerne Abbas by Benjamin Pryce, 1768

Everson, P. L., Taylor, C. C., & Dunn, C. J. 1991 *Change and Continuity, Rural Settlement in North-West Lincolnshire* RCHME

Gibbons, A.O. 1962 *Cerne Abbas*

Hutchins, J. 1870 *The History and Antiquities of the County of Dorset Vol. IV*, (3 edn)

National Monuments Record Centre (NMR), NMR no ST 60 SE 41, Kemble Drive, Swindon

Pattison, P. Field, D. & Ainsworth, S. (eds) 1999 *Patterns of the Past, Essays in Landscape Archaeology for Christopher Taylor*

Royal Commission on Historical Monuments (England), 1952 *An Inventory of the Historical Monuments in Dorset: Vol. I West*

Riley, H. & Wilson-North, R. 1999 'From Pillow Mounds to Parterres: a revelation at Cerne Abbas' in Pattison, P. *et al* (eds), 71–6

Taylor, C. C. 1970 *Dorset*

Taylor, C. C. 1991 'Introduction', in *Garden Archaeology*, (ed.) A. E. Brown, CBA Research Report no 78, 1–5

Taylor, C. C. 1994 'The regular village plan: Dorset revisited and revised', in *The Medieval Landscape of Wessex*, (eds) M. Aston & C. Lewis, Oxbow Monograph 46, 213–18

Victoria History of the County of Dorset, 1908 Vol. II The Religious Houses of Dorset

Victoria History of the County of Dorset, 1968 Vol. III Domesday Survey

Roman Forts in a Designed Landscape. East Holton, Wareham St Martin, Dorset: A Journey to Cuckoo-Land

Ian Hewitt and Eileen Wilkes

Introduction

This paper documents the implications of some preliminary investigations into the history of eighteenth- and nineteenth-century woodland enclosures in Dorset. The work was instigated as a development of a larger enterprise entitled 'The Early History of the English Channel Project' (EHECP), a joint venture between Bournemouth University and the University of Southampton. In simple terms, the aim is to map the pattern and development of human exploitation of the coastline and littoral of the English Channel. Poole Harbour was identified as a key area of study. By chance, the Trustees of the Holton Lee Estate (East Holton) which includes a Site of Special Scientific Interest (SSSI), contacted the authors with a view to achieving a greater understanding of a number of sites on their land. This proposal was in line with the Trust's educational objectives. The Trustees were anxious to know more about a rectilinear enclosure

that had been identified as a possible Roman fort with an associated military road (Field, 1992). On its part, Bournemouth University was keen to negotiate a survey of the littoral of the Estate in support of the EHECP research objectives. An agreement was reached and an initial three-week evaluation programme was arranged for July 2000. An investigation of the supposed Roman fort and its subsequent ramifications are the subject of this paper.

The Context

Enclosure A

In 1992 N.H. Field set out the evidence for a Roman road from Lake Farm, Corfe Mullen (NGR 400000 099000), the site of a major Roman military base, to Wareham (NGR 392350 087400). A stretch of this 14km route was believed to cross Holton Heath on a line almost parallel with the A 351, the modern Poole to Wareham road, but a little less than 1km to the south-east of it. Field proposed that two rectilinear earthworks on the Holton Lee Estate (Fig. 49, A and B) were Roman forts associated with the road (Field 1992, 143–8). The existence of such a road, if proved, would have major implications for the archaeology of Wareham, a town set out around a cruciform road system contained within west, north and east earth bank walls. These features are characteristics of some Roman towns but archaeological evidence of this period is not plentiful at Wareham. The presence of a Roman road from Lake Farm to Wareham would dispel the lingering doubts regarding the town's antiquity. Field's Enclosure A was chosen for the initial investigation for reason of its close proximity to the conjectural Roman road.

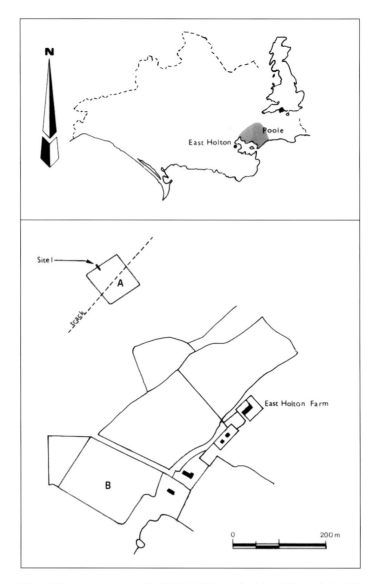

Fig. 49 Location plans (after Field, 1992 and with additional details)

Site Inspection and Survey

The Holton Lee Estate is at the eastern end of Wareham St Martin Parish. The whole of the parish comprises acid heathland soils over Bagshot Beds (RCHME 1970, 326). Initial site inspection of the Estate revealed a heathland environment with residual plantations of conifer trees. Mature deciduous trees form a boundary between the heathland and the reed beds of the Lytchett Bay (Poole Harbour) shoreline. Shallow ditches traverse much of the Estate and these comprise a derelict irrigation and land reclamation system for which there is evidence of at least two phases. This is a post-medieval designed landscape. The supposed Roman fort is in an area of cleared conifer plantation where re-colonisation by appropriate flora and fauna demonstrates the success of the Trust's heathland regeneration programme.

Site inspection of Field's Enclosure A revealed it as a rectilinear earthwork situated on open heathland approximately 400m north-west of East Holton Farm (NGR 396000 091700). A stand of coniferous trees lies within 100m to the south and the canalised River Sherford flows eastwards into Lytchett Bay 500m north and east of the site. The Enclosure A earthworks comprise an external ditch with an inner bank enclosing 0.6ha, or approximately 1½ acres. Field's sketch plan of the enclosure shows it as having rounded corners and this would have been consistent with the form of a Roman military camp (Field 1992, 144–5). A vehicle trackway flanked by fire break ditches now cuts across the enclosure from south-east to north-west and this disturbance, Field argued, could have been responsible for obliterating important features such as original enclosure entrances. In addition, forestry ploughing and drainage leats have been responsible for extensive ground disturbance across most of the heath including the interior of Enclosure A.

Historical Background

There are few remaining Estate archives for East Holton and a desk-based assessment produced a limited amount of historical evidence. Holton is listed in the Dorset Domesday Book (Morris (ed.) 1983) as a small estate of half a hide. The entry does not distinguish between 'East' and 'West' Holton and so it is probable that the Domesday holding was sub-divided at a later date. Mills (1998, 88–9) suggests that the place-name might derive from Old English *holt*, a wood, and a few substantial oaks still stand close to the shoreline. The Royal Commission on Historical Monuments confirms the antiquity of the estate but has nothing else to add (1970, 326). Enclosure A is not shown on the Tithe Map for Wareham St Martin (DRO 1843) but it was included on the first edition of the Ordnance Survey six-inch County Series map (*c.*1870). It therefore seemed probable that Enclosure A was created at some time between these two dates, i.e. during the mid nineteenth century, and was therefore not a Roman fort.

Excavation

Method

Our initial view was that Enclosure A was a component of the post-medieval landscape but in order to determine the date, structure and purpose of the feature, limited archaeological excavation was necessary. With the aim of deriving the maximum amount of information with the minimum destruction, a single trench, 1.5m wide and 7.1m in length, was cut across the ditch and bank on the north-west side of the enclosure (Fig. 49, Site 1). Hand tools were used throughout. The position of the trench was adjacent to a section of the enclosure bank that had been previously damaged during the process of recent conifer tree clearance.

Results

The excavation revealed a shallow enclosure ditch of 0.55m depth and 1.45m width. The north side of the ditch comprised a series of four shallow steps, typically with risers of 0.1m and treads of 0.25m (Fig. 50). These steps have been interpreted as spade cuts. Spoil from the digging of the ditch had been cast southwards

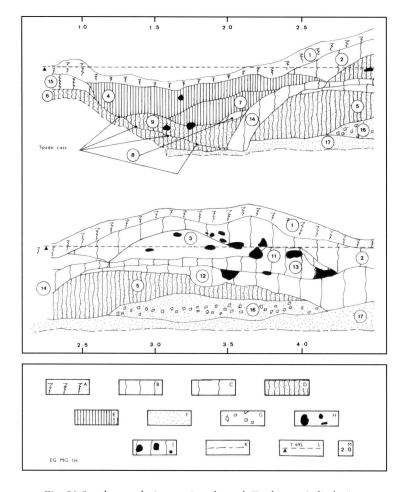

Fig. 50 South-west facing section through Enclosure A ditch. A =
topsoil, B = sandy loam, C = loamy sand, D = sandy clay loam, E =
loam, F = sand, G = sand with pebble inclusions, H = surface stones, J
= grit stones within sandy loam matrix, K = extent of excavation, L =
datum line (7.695m), M = Section measurements in 0.5m gradations

to form a shallow internal bank. At present, the bank measures approximately 2m wide (north-south) and 0.3m high, but this does not allow for spread and it is probable that the original height of the bank was close to 0.5m (i.e. equal to the depth of the ditch).

The section through the bank revealed a stratigraphy that included some lumps of gritty stone at the base close to the south end (Fig. 50). These stones varied in size from 0.1m x 0.1m down to examples less than half that size. All appeared blackened as if burned but there

was no evidence of associated charcoal. The presence of the gritty stones was attributed not to human deposition but rather to natural formation by the process of cementation (Beavis pers. comm.).

The shape of the ditch was unlike those that are found on Roman camps and forts. These would normally have been V-shape in profile with a slot cut into the bottom (Webster 1985, 177; Putnam, pers. comm.) whereas the Enclosure A ditch was gently rounded and without a slot. In addition, a palisade might be expected on the bank of a Roman camp but there was no evidence for such a feature at Enclosure A.

Chronology

No artefacts of any period were recovered from the trench and no casual surface finds have been reported. However, Enclosure A possessed no defensive potential and its characteristics indicated that it is a comparatively modern feature. Other clues reinforce this conclusion. The preliminary site inspection had revealed that the corners of the enclosure are not distinctly rounded in the Roman 'playing card' style as indicated by Field (1992, 145), but upon each of the bank's corners a low mound can be seen. These are known as corner mounds and they are typical of eighteenth- and nineteenth-century woodland enclosures. Such mounds were formed when spoil from conjoining sections of ditch became heaped up at one point (Rackham 1993, 114–6). The corner mounds of Enclosure A had become slightly spread and this might have persuaded Field that the corners were deliberately rounded. In essence, there was nothing in the excavation results that confounded the evidence of the desk-based assessment.

Developments

The results of the survey and excavation of Enclosure A provided a springboard for further investigation. We can now regard Enclosure A as a component of the post-medieval designed landscape of the Holton Estate and with this in mind, a search for similar Dorset silviculture enclosures was initiated. One of those identified is a lozenge-shape feature of *c*.0.9ha on Canford Heath, Poole (NGR 402900 096100). This enclosure is marked upon the 1997 Ordnance Survey Explorer map but it is otherwise undocumented. A better known example is on the south side of Eggardon hillfort in Askerswell CP which has an unusual polygonal shape and

it is generally thought to have been a navigation aid for offshore shipping (Royal Commission on Historical Monuments (England) 1952, 14 & 15). The Eggardon enclosure has become the subject of folklore and legend for it is popularly asserted that it was created by a notorious Dorset smuggler, Issac Gulliver, to convenience his trade in contraband goods. The truth of this story is open to doubt but nevertheless, folk associations with woodland enclosures are known and Harte (1986, 29–30) claims to have identified nine enclosures that are variously known as *cuckoo pounds*, *cuckoo pens* or similar. These names are included in Table 1 together with Dorset Cuckoo place-names derived from the Dorset Record Office (1998), the Dorset Environmental Records Centre (DERC) and cartographic survey.

Enclosure Size

The Canford Heath, East Holton and Eggardon enclosures are not known to be 'cuckoo-' name sites but they are sufficiently similar to some of those in Table 1 that they require inclusion. In fact, they simply add to the diversity of the group. In shape, East Holton and Canford Heath are similar to the Langton Matravers enclosure, whilst the polygon at Eggardon has no parallel within the group. It is difficult to compare enclosure size because neither Harte nor DERC were concerned with this detail. Canford Heath (*c*.2¼ statute acres), East Holton (*c*.1½ statute acres) and Langton Matravers (a little over 1½ statute acres) are quadrilaterals and their respective areas suggest random measurements. It is possible that size was calculated in customary rather than in statute acres but these local units of measurements could vary from parish to parish or even from one manor to the next. The most obvious examples of such variations can be found in the Tithe Apportionments where a field called, say, Seven Acres, might have been measured as either more or less than seven statute acres and recorded thus in the statute acres column. Virtually no work has been carried out on customary units of measurements in Dorset but research has taken

Table 1: Known 'Cuckoo-' place-name sites in Dorset

	Parish	Cuckoo-name	NGR	Details
1	Arne*	Goocroft or Cuckoo-croft	Not given	Field-name. No other details.
2	Bere Regis*+	Cuckoo Pound	386600 090400	Plantation near to Newfoundland Farm.
3	Bradford Peverell*+	Cuckoo Pond / Pound / Plot / Pen	367000 092400	Island (irregular) used as a plantation. Formerly in Charminster CP.
4	Chalbury*+	Cuckoo Pound	400000 107100	A plantation of this name in 1888. Also listed as Crichel and Witchampton. Near to New Town.
5	Church Knowle+	Cuckoo Ground	391300 082700	Near to Creech Heath.
6	Coombe Keynes+	Cuckoo Nod and Mini Nod	384300 084200	Two Cottages in Coombe Keynes sharing one run of thatch.
7	Corfe Castle*+	Cuckoo Pen	397800 085500	Circular woodland enclosure. On Rempstone Heath.
8	Frampton*	Cuckoo Pen	not given	Plot with 2 cottages.
9	Langton Matravers*	Cuckoo Pound	400800 077600	An irregular quadrilateral woodland enclosure.
10	Lulworth*+	Cuckoo Pound	386600 083200	Wood near to Lulworth Heath. Near to New Barn Plantation and Botany Farm. Alternatively listed as East Lulworth.
11	Poole ~	Cuckoo Lane	403460 093900 to 403750 093670	In Newtown suburb. Leads onto Mannings Heath.
12	Ryme Intrinsica+	Cuckoo Hill	358200 109300 to 358500 109200	A hill.
13	Steeple*+	Cuckoo Pound	388900 080500	An oval enclosure. Also listed as Tyneham.
14	Stinsford+	Cuckoo Lane	372300 092200 to 372500 092900	Lane flanked by small holdings south of Higher Bockhampton Farm.
15	Thorncombe+	Cuckoo Lane	338700 104000 to 338800 103900	A lane. Also listed as Southcombe.
16	Wareham, Lady St Mary+	Cuckoo Lane	391300 087000 to 391600 086500	A lane on Wareham Common, now mostly destroyed. Also listed as Worgret.
17	Wareham, Dollins Lane, Lady St Mary ~	Cuckoo Pound	392350 088560	Quadrilateral enclosure with cottage (now a bungalow).

Sites identified by: Harte; DERC+; Authors~

place in Sussex and Hampshire. Pile (2000a, 32–5) has examined the Tithe Map data for the Bedhampton, Havant and Farlington parishes and manors of Hampshire and this has indicated a customary acre size of 0.64 to 0.67 statute acres within his survey area. Such figures cannot be applied to Dorset but it is clear that there needs to be research on customary measures in the County and that their application to medieval and post-medieval features such as silvicultural enclosures needs to be considered.

Sivicultural Enclosures and 'Cuckoo' Place-Names

Harte (1986) believed that his investigations into the Dorset 'cuckoo-' enclosures revealed two common factors. First, the name was associated with earthworks that surrounded stands of trees. Second, that the name was applied to sites in the eighteenth-century. How-

ever, it is also obvious that there is much variation within the data set if it is taken on its face value. Amongst Harte's six sites that he confidently associates with silviculture, two (Lulworth and Chalbury) are said to be plantations with no enclosure implied. At Bradford Peverell, an island in the River Frome was used as an ash plantation. The example at Arne, 'Goocroft' (Cuckoo-croft), was a field-name that might have been associated with a wood or coppice but the '-croft' element suggests an enclosure associated with a building or small holding. The Corfe Castle and Tyneham examples are described as 'circular' and 'oval', arousing the suspicion that they might be monuments of a more ancient date later re-used as plantation enclosures. Only Langton Matravers is described as a quadrilateral woodland enclosure similar to those at East Holton and at Canford Heath. Taking a broader view than Harte, the Wareham Cuckoo Pound and the Frampton Cuckoo Pen are certainly associated with buildings within a plot. Other sites are described as 'lanes' (e.g. Poole) or a 'hill' (Ryme Intrinsica). From this diversity it is clear that the association of

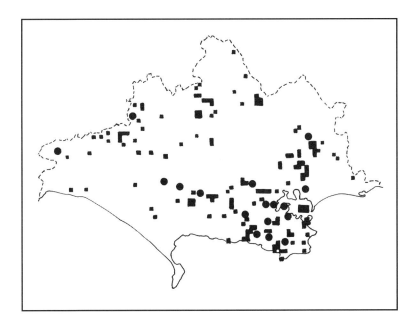

Fig. 51 Distribution map of 'cuckoo' place-names and cuckoo habitat in Dorset. Squares represent 1km² within which a cuckoo was detected; circles represent known 'cuckoo-' place-names

'cuckoo-' place-names with woodland plant-ations is not proven (Table 1 above).

Distribution

The occurrence of 'cuckoo-' place-names might be expected to be coincident with the distribution of the habitat of the bird, and there is some evidence to support this hypothesis. Figures for cuckoo distribution are available for Dorset for the years 1985 and 1986 (Anon. 1987). These figures relate to male birds only because they can be identified by their distinctive call. The survey for 1985 shows two fairly consistent concentrations, one in the south-east, the other across the north of the county (Fig. 51). The cuckoos' range was wider in 1986 but the overall pattern has important similarities to that of the previous year. Of the total number of 17 known 'cuckoo' place-names in Table 1, 15 are clustered in the south-east of Dorset. This area of the greatest concentration of 'cuckoo' place-names, is one of clays, sands and heaths. In the last 200 years the south-east of Dorset has become noted for its plantations of conifers, a habitat that might be regarded as attractive cover for the cuckoo. Clays are also a feature of north and west Dorset where the remaining two 'cuckoo-' place-names can be found (Ryme Intrinsica and Thorncombe).

The Cuckoo in Dorset Folklore

Bond (1975, 112) cites an instance in which the cuckoo plays a part in Dorset folklore. Here, the bird was supposed to have visited Wareham Fair, according to Owen on 7th April (1756, 29), in order to buy breeches. Harte (1986, 29), using an unspecified source, expands upon the Wareham Fair story declaring that the wise men of the town attributed the backwardness of the season to the late arrival of the cuckoo. Consequently, a plan was devised to fence in the cuckoo (i.e. to enclose or pen the bird) so that it should become a permanent resident. Conceivably, the essence of this story is preserved in a Wareham property deed (DRO 1910) that relates to a plot at the corner of Dollings Lane ". . . formerly known as 'The Cuckoo Pound'". Unfortunately, there is no evidence of there having been a pound (i.e. enclosure or pen) on this site. Notes that accompany a late eighteenth-century four-part map of Wareham (DRO *c*.1790) indicate that a house and garden occupied the site of this cuckoo pound, a reference that is supported by the Tithe Apportionment for the parish of Wareham St Mary that refers to it as a garden. The accompanying Tithe Map shows that there was a cottage or house in that garden (DRO 1838). From this one might infer that either the 1910 deed is mistaken, or that the name 'Cuckoo Pound' had been transferred

Table 2: Known 'Cuckoo-' place-name sites in Hampshire

	Approximate Location	Cuckoo-name	Details
1	Bransgore	Cuckoo Hill Lane	Leads onto the Common.
2	Chandlers Ford	Cuckoo Bushes Lane	In the suburb of Cuckoo Bushes and parallel with Common Road.
3	Gorley	Cuckoo Hill	An enclosure in the New Forest.
4	North Waltham	Cuckoo Close	Probably twentieth-century.
5	Southampton	Cuckoo Lane	Hugs the line of the medieval town wall.
6	Titchfield	Cuckoo Road	Stubbington.

All sites identified by Authors from road maps

to this plot from a nearby site. Alternatively, the evidence from Wareham suggests that 'cuckoo-' place-names were not confined to silvicultural enclosures but also to garden plots and that the legend of the penning of the cuckoo has no obvious association with the Wareham Cuckoo Pound.

Other Cuckoo Place-Names

Place-name etymologists have conspired against the cuckoo. Mills (1998) lists no 'cuckoo-' place-names in Dorset although there are at least 17 (Table 1). They are also absent from Ekwall (1960) and from Room's useful work on modern place-names (1983). However, it is important to urge caution, for the majority of place-name books are concerned with settlement names only and minor names, such as those of coppices and fields are excluded. Even so, the exclusion of the cuckoo is a matter for concern and its omission is not confined to Dorset. Room (1992) gives no examples of urban cuckoo-names but there is a Cuckoo Lane within the town walls of medieval Southampton. Similarly, Coates (1989) lists no cuckoo sites for Hampshire although a survey of road maps indicates that they occur at Bransgore, Chandlers Ford, Gorley and Stubbington (Table 2). Most of these places are in south-west Hampshire, virtually adjacent to the principal Dorset concentration. Their omission from place-name surveys is a bar to understanding why cuckoo-names were applied, and when. Cunliffe inadvertently shows the way forward. He describes the Hampshire home of the early twentieth-century archaeologist Heywood Sumner as being at, "Cuckoo Hill near Gorley . . . within the boundaries of the New Forest. When he (Sumner) saw it (in 1902), Cuckoo Hill was simply a plot of land- 'a squatter's holding on the gravel hills of the Forest . . .' " (1985, 11). Sumner's Cuckoo Hill closely resembles some of the Dorset cuckoo-sites described above, an enclosure or plot probably associated with woodland. However, the key word in the description of Cuckoo Hill is 'squatter'. Richards defines 'squatter' as "a per-

son who encloses common land and builds on it without permission of the manor court" (1986, 19). The association of the cuckoo with a squatter plot at Gorley is important for in this sense the breeding habit of the cuckoo, occupation of another bird's nest and resources, can be seen as synonymous with the illegal land grabbing of the squatter. 'Cuckoo' was being used as a metaphor for 'squatter'. 'Cuckoo Pound /Pen' (or whatever) belongs to the same group of derisive post-medieval place-names such as 'Turkey Island' which refers to a community of squatter holdings in Shedfield Parish, Hampshire. Here, the word 'turk' refers to a lawless community (Pile 2000b) probably in the sense that its members are acting against the authority of the manor court.

'Cuckoo' place-names can be associated with woodland enclosures on the commons and some of these may have been set out as a result of a perceived shortage in navy ship building timber towards the end of the eighteenth-century (Stagg 1989). Universal application of this very specific interpretation is not supported by the facts and it seems that the term 'cuckoo' came to apply to any enclosure established upon the common land either with or without a building. There seems to have been no original building at Sumner's 'Cuckoo Hill' for the house of this name was constructed after his purchase of the site (Cunliffe 1985, 11). The Cuckoo Pound within the town of Wareham was not a silvicultural enclosure but the deed of 1910 implies that it was a squatter house built within a plot owned by the Rempstone Estate (DRO 1910). Cuckoo lanes would therefore imply route ways flanked by squatter holdings such as that at Higher Bockhampton (Stinsford, Dorset). Table 1 shows that most of the 'cuckoo'- sites are either on former common lands, such as heathlands, or alongside lanes that gave access to these areas. Frequently, cuckoo-sites have associated place-names. In Poole, Cuckoo Lane is in Newtown, whilst the Cuckoo Lane in Bere Regis is at New Town. These names are indicative of new settlement areas (squats). Cuckoo Pound, in Lulworth, is close to Botany, an appropriate name for newly cultivated fields that are hard to work.

Taking the above into account, the authors propose that three criteria determined the origin of a 'cuckoo'- place-name:

1. The site needed to be on the common land, probably the common wastes such as heathland and roadside verges.
2. The site was occupied without the permission of the manor court.
3. The site was generally within, or near to, the breeding grounds of the cuckoo

Discussion

The Holton Enclosures

As a result of our investigations we can demonstrate that Field's Enclosure A at East Holton is between 150 and 200 years old. It was created within the heathland in order to mark out an area for growing trees. These trees have since been felled and the original use of the enclosure has been forgotten. The reclassification of Enclosure A as a post-medieval silvicultural enclosure undermines Field's case for an associated Roman road from Lake Farm to Wareham. The road could have existed without a Roman fort in this area and the conjectural course of this road is a separate issue that remains to be tested. Field's Enclosure B, likewise classified by him as a Roman fort, also demands attention. These matters will be on the agenda for the 2001 season.

'Cuckoo'- Place-names and the Designed Landscape

The re-assessment of Field's original hypothesis for Enclosure A moved this small component of the EHECP from Roman forts onto post-medieval woodland enclosures, and onwards to an investigation into the origin of 'cuckoo-' place-names. Other silvicultural enclosures of the East Holton type remain to be identified in Dorset and elsewhere (Brown M. 1995, 17) but fieldwork and desk-based research has indicated that they vary in size, shape and date. The authors have found no examples that occur within a designed landscape of the scale of East Holton, but extensive fieldwork remains to be undertaken.

What does seem certain is that 'cuckoo-' place-names are chronologically co-terminous with late medieval and post-medieval re-organization of the rural landscape. It is also clear that 'cuckoo' sites were not a planned component of a much broader and more sophisticated scheme. Instead, they signal the location of opportunistic appendages to landscape designs by squatter communities that had the imagination and determination to exploit these developments and the loosening of residual feudal ties. At Boarhunt (pronounced 'Burrant'), Hampshire, a squatter community developed along the western margin of *Trampers'* Lane, a routeway onto a former area of heathland that had been carved up into rectilinear closes and made ready for managed agricultural production (Hewitt, 2002). Boarhunt demonstrates the blurred distinction between official and unofficial aspects of designed landscapes whereby the two were virtually complimentary and inter-dependent. Enclosure A at East Holton can be seen in this context. It was constructed at a time when a major land improvement scheme was draining the marshy hinterland of the river Sherford, slicing off significant bends in the watercourse, and cutting new leats to speed the delivery of ground water from the heathlands into Lytchett Bay. It is not yet possible to be certain whether Enclosure A was an integral part of the whole scheme, or whether it was an opportunistic unofficial add-on.

Implications and Opportunities

'Cuckoo-' place-names are a helpful dating tool because they represent one of a group of similar names that are synonymous with post-medieval squatter establishments on heaths and commons. The field at Arne, Dorset, is the only known site that takes the Old English form *gowk* in preference to the Middle English *cuckoo* (Brown L. 1993). However, it is far more likely that the use of the Old English equivalent is indicative of a local dialect survival rather than the earlier application of 'cuckoo' as a place-name element. In the chronological sense Harte was correct when he ascribed 'cuckoo-' names to the eighteenth or nineteenth centuries, but he was wrong to assume that all 'cuckoo-' place-names were associated with woodland enclosures. It has been demonstrated that some 'cuckoo-' sites contained squatter cottages and we are reminded by Crossley (1990, 41) that there is a lack of post-medieval evidence for the homes of the very poor in rural England. It is important that 'cuckoo-' sites should be sub-classified into settlement and non-settlement types, for some of the former will contain the evidence of occupation that we seek. In short, the scope, purpose and origin of post-medieval enclosures is an archaeological challenge that is worthy of further attention.

Update

Since this paper was written, there have been two significant developments in the Poole Harbour heathlands. In March 2001 Poole Borough Council obtained consent to close Cuckoo Lane. Historically it was an important route that linked the manorial pound at Newtown with Mannings Heath. At much the same time, the Tomorrow's Heathland Heritage programme was launched, coincidentally, at East Holton. The initiative aims to link a number of disparate parcels of heathland by the creation of land corridors. In this way it is hoped to restore much of the lost and degraded heathland environment of east Dorset and west Hampshire. This project amounts to a reversal of eighteenth and nineteenth century designed landscape schemes that contrived to make these infertile soils productive. It is a matter of conjecture as to whether the aim of the project can be achieved without significant interference (destruction) with designed landscape features.

Acknowledgements

Our thanks to the Trustees and staff of the Holton Lee Estate and to our colleagues John Beavis and Bill Putnam for their helpful interpretative comments regarding the soils and Roman forts respectively. Emma Graham and Michael Green excavated Enclosure A at East Holton and produced the section drawing reproduced as Fig. 50. Finally, we recognise with gratitude the work of the late Norman Field whose hypotheses about the archaeology of East Holton have led to new avenues of study.

References

Anon. 1987 'Cuckoo Survey' *Proceedings of the Dorset Natural History and Archaeological Society* 108, 220–1

Bond, L. 1956 *Tyneham, A Lost Heritage* (Second Edition)

Brown, L. (ed.) *The New Shorter Oxford English Dictionary*

Brown, M. 1995 *The Gazetteer of Dartmoor Names*

Coates, R. 1989 *The Place-names of Hampshire*

Crossley, D. 1990 *Post-medieval Archaeology in Britain*

Cunliffe, B. 1985 *Heywood Sumner's Wessex*

DERC 1998 *A Gazetteer of Dorset Place-names: a Supplement*, Dorset Environmental Records Centre

Dorset Environmental Records Centre 1998 *A Gazetteer of Dorset Place-names*

D/FIL: /T33 1910 Deed of Land called the Cuckoo Pound, in Dollings Lane, Dorset County Record Office

DI/LX 38/1 1838 Wareham St Mary Tithe Map, Dorset County Record Office

D/RWR: E53 *c*.1790 Map of Wareham in four parts with notes up to 1812, Dorset County Record Office

Ekwall, E. 1960 *The Concise Oxford Dictionary of Place-names* (Fourth Edition)

Field, N.H. 1992 *Dorset and the Second Legion*

Harte, J. 1986 *Cuckoo Pounds and Singing Barrows*

Hewitt, I. 2000 Site One: The Enclosure In Eileen Wilkes and Ian Hewitt *Poole Harbour Littoral: The Holton Lee Project 2000* (Bournemouth University School of Conservation Sciences Research Report 8) Bournemouth, Bournemouth University

Hewitt, I. 2002 *Historic Rural Settlement in the Winchester City District, Hampshire* (Commissioned report for Hampshire County Council)

Mills, A.D. 1998 *Dorset Place-names, Their Origin and Meaning*

Morris, J. (ed.) 1983 *Domesday Book: Dorset*

Owen, W. 1756 *The Book of Fairs*

Pile, J. 2000a 'The Customary Acre in South Hampshire' *Hampshire Field Club & Archaeological Society Newsletter* 34, 32–5

Pile, J. 2000b 'Talking Turkey' *Hampshire Field Club & Archaeological Society Newsletter* 33, 7–8

Richardson, J. 1986 *The Local Historian's Encyclopaedia*

Room, A. 1983 *A Concise Dictionary of Modern Place-Names in Great Britain and Ireland*

Room, A. 1992 *The Street Names of England*

Rackham, O. 1993 *Trees and Woodland in the British Countryside*

Royal Commission on Historical Monuments (England) 1952 *An Inventory of the Historical Monuments in Dorset* I

Royal Commission on Historical Monuments (England) 1970 *An Inventory of the Historical Monuments in Dorset* II, 2

Stagg, D.J. 1989 'Silvicultural Inclosure in the New Forest to 1870' *Proceedings of the Hampshire Field Club and Archaeological Society, 135–45.*

TWA (SM) 1843–4 Wareham St Martin Tithe Map and Apportionment, Dorset County Record Office

The Downes, Hayle

June Fenwick

Introduction

The gardens at The Downes, Hayle might be referred to as a walled secret garden containing a house. It is unique in Cornwall and may well be so in the United Kingdom. The Downes occupies an elevated position on the outskirts of Hayle next to St Michael's Hospital Hayle with grounds sloping north and west. It is evident that this was to enjoy the prospect of fine views, north-west over the Hayle Estuary to the church of St Uny Lelant, and west to the hills of Trencrom and Trink. The history of Downes allowed the property to slip gently into obscurity until in November 1994 the garden was spot registered by English Heritage. The Cornwall Gardens Trust were then asked to record the garden land as a matter of urgency. The English Heritage registration was prompted by a planning application for a car park within the walled garden for use by the adjoining hospital.

History

The original owner, Mr W.J. Rawlings of Hayle, decided to build a new house and gave the contract to John D. Sedding, an architect. It is

probable he gave Sedding complete authority and funds to match. The materials throughout house and garden are of the highest quality, local Elvan and Breage granite and the geometric design and measurements of terraces, paths and walls were precisely executed.

Sedding (1838–1891) was the younger brother of Edmund Sedding, an architect who retired to Penzance for his health in 1865. John Sedding joined his brother in designing and laying out The Downes in 1867. Edmund died in 1868 and John carried on after his death. John D. Sedding later became well known in the 1880s as a founder member of the Art Worker's Guild, described as a blend of academic artists with revolutionary architects and designers. His Cornish church restorations and decorative interiors are listed in Pevsner Radcliffe as including St Elwyn, Hayle and All Saints, Falmouth. The influences that guided his work on Downes were his beliefs in a Gothic Revival and in the growth of the Arts and Crafts style. In 1887 an article in *The British Architect* entitled 'A Ramble in West Cornwall' described the integration of house and garden in glowing terms: 'The Arts and Crafts ideal "natural house set in a formal landscape"'.

W.E. Lethaby writing an obituary 'A note on the artistic life and work of John D. Sedding' in *The Builder* October 10th 1891, makes no mention of Downes or other domestic architecture by Sedding. There were thoughts of Sedding's love of poetry and music and the books he preferred being herbals and natural histories, including the authors Gerard and Bewick and Curtis's *Botanical Magazine*.

In 1891 a group of Sedding's friends posthumously published *Garden Craft Old and New*, a work Sedding had completed in October 1890. It was a collection of his thoughts and sketches on the subject and included phrases such as 'a garden that curtseys to the house with its formal lines, its terraces and beds of geometrical patterns'. The book went into three printings and possibly exerted considerable influence on the development of the Aesthetic style.

William. J. Rawlings and his wife died in the early 1890s. In 1901 the estate was bought by a Miss Frances Ellis, a wealthy Catholic, in order to bestow it on a community of nuns, the Order of the Daughters of the Cross of Liege.

Their Chaplain, the Reverend Mullins in his unpublished volume 'Rambles in West Cornwall' written in 1915, describes the garden as

Fig. 52 View from the gravel terrace along the central axis to the northern boundary (© June Fenwick)

six acres of land, tastefully laid out in terrace walks, lawns, shrubberies, kitchen and flower gardens. The house and grounds had engaged, during many years, the constant solicitude of the owner and originator, Mr W.J. Rawlings; and though a few years of neglect had passed upon them between the date of his death and the arrival of the nuns, no irreparable damage had ensued.

Mullins refers to one ambition of Mr Rawlings to 'equal or surpass his neighbours in the variety and rarity of the plants and trees in his collection'.

The House and Garden

St Michael's Hospital was built on the east side of the original designed Downes landscape and the present entrance to the house is a drive from the B3302 Hayle to Helston road through the hospital area. The wooden carriage gates in the east boundary wall lead into a walled courtyard on the east side of the house. The courtyard is gravelled with beds of mixed shrubs and climbers on the north and east walls. In the northeastern corner of the courtyard walls a door leads through to the main garden.

The garden is to the north and east of the house with a gravelled terrace running along the north face of the house acting as a pivotal feature. On the east end of the top terrace a decorative summerhouse with doors painted green and white is built into the east wall. An interesting internal feature is an "eyrie" (possibly for owner or gardener to view the garden). The construction is of random stone with dressed stone surrounds and a hipped slate roof.

To the north of this main terrace the garden slopes down in a series of terraces or levels with a strong axial path leading from the garden entrance of the house down a series of flights of steps between the levels to terminate in a stone arbour, known as 'St Germoe's Chair'. To the south of the terrace on the west front of the house is a square lawn and to the west of this, stretching the whole length of the formal garden, is an informal area that was formerly orchards and now in part is the burial ground for the Sisters.

Between the west lawn and the informal area is a bank formerly planted with rare shrubs but now mainly grassed. The gravel path bordering the bank, running north to south, possibly ended in an ornamental gate of which only one iron post now remains.

The main terrace along the north front of the house runs east west for approximately 80 yards, in depth 10 yards. The balustrade or wall on the north side of the top terrace is pierced at regular intervals by trefoil headed openings. The construction is of random moor stone with Polyphant stone capping. The planting on the terrace consisted of a series of small round and square beds, 7 of each, bordered with chamfered grey bricks made from refuse china clay. These were originally planted alternately with hollies and yews clipped into formal shapes. From the north side of the main terrace, opposite the garden entrance to the house a flight of eight granite steps leads down to the next level known as the 'geometric garden' bisected by the central path. This garden is now laid out to grass with a narrow border bed on either side of the central path. At this time annual bedding in a formal design is being used in the border

to convey some idea of the original colour and shape.

The original design was influenced by a Heidelberg garden layout by Solomon Caus in 1623. *The British Architect* states it was laid out by Sedding. The geometric garden is about two-thirds the length of the main terrace and the other third is taken up by an area of trees with winding paths. Originally here were small parterre beds bordered with box, not bricks. There is now no trace.

The central axis of the garden continues from the geometric garden level down a double flight of eleven granite steps to the yew lawn level. Originally this was bordered by 'twenty-two Irish yews about fifteen feet in height'. The present surviving trees are in poor condition and are being cut hard back to stimulate regrowth. On both sides of the path are level lawns which on the east side are now covered by construction work cabins for the hospital extensions. This is to be restored.

Although some of the original planting of holly and yew trees remain on the western edge, many have not survived. A narrow path running south to north divides these trees from an area now planted with young eucalyptus trees. This area now extends into the Old Orchard area which it is hoped can be restored as an orchard. Towards the western boundaries on this level

Fig. 53 Summerhouse built into the east end wall of the top terrace
(© June Fenwick)

Fig. 54 East face of arbour St Germoe's Chair
(© June Fenwick)

is the Burial ground laid out by the Community in the twentieth century.

A third flight of five steps northwards on the main axis path between low hedged banks leads down to a cross walk dividing the formal gardens from the flower and walled vegetable garden. A further three granite steps continue down to a northwards path bordered by yew, finishing at a stone arbor built in imitation of St Germoe's Chair. The Chair stands over a cross-axis east to west path. The original stands in St Germoe's churchyard.

To the east and west of the arbor, on the boundary walls to the north and east are the marks of the former peach houses. The walled area has been used to grow shrubs, plants and vegetables to supply the Community. Some of the original glass and potting sheds on the north-west of this area remain, together with a new greenhouse replacement.

On the north side of the original potting sheds, a brick wall separates them from the Head Gardener's cottage which has access to the north boundary drive. Remains of the buildings used formerly as a school by the Community are in the north-west corner. As an example

of John D Sedding's philosophy The Downes house and garden are quite literally unique.

Postscript

At the time of going to press, the property has been sold to a private buyer.

References

Anon 'A Ramble in West Cornwall' in *The British Architect*, 16th December 1887, 443–8

Cornwall Gardens Trust 1995 Garden Record Cornwall Record Office x897/17

Daughters of the Cross of Liege (descriptive booklet undated)

Hunt and Pett, D.D. 1991 *Historic Gardens of Cornwall*

Lethaby, W.E. 1891 'A note on the artistic life and work of John Sedding' in *The Builder* October 10th 1891

Mullins, Rev. T. 1915 'Rambles in West Cornwall Vol. 1' (unpub.)

Pevsner, N. *The Buildings of England, Falmouth and Hayle*, 67 and 80

Prospectus *Daughters of the Cross Downes* (undated)

Sedding, J.D. 1891 *Garden Craft Old and New*

Fig. 55 View north west over the Hayle estuary
(© June Fenwick)

The Walled Garden at Churchtown, Morval

Alison A. Newton

Setting

Churchtown lies within a small south-facing valley not far from the River Looe. The site is approached through a deep, narrow and probably ancient lane from the village of Morval. Churchtown House has been created from three cottages and is situated at the lowest part of the garden, adjacent to the church of St Wenna. Morval House, which was the manor of the Morval Estate, lies just beyond the church. It was sold in 1973 and is now separate from the estate.

History

The Morval estate was owned by the Buller family from the late seventeenth century until 1900 when it passed to the four daughters of the Buller family. One of these daughters married into the Tremayne family from Heligan, and the Tremaynes occupied the house from 1900–1940. It then passed to John Buller's grandson, Captain J. B. Kitson R.N., who died in 1976. The present property of Churchtown was part of the large Morval estate until 1960.

Several maps of the estate, and also detailed records of land use dating from the eighteenth century, show that the area now known as Churchtown was used for fruit and vegetable production, although the meadow adjacent to the property was described as *arboretum* on the tithe map of 1846. Some of this land may have been leased in separate holdings. At that time, a kitchen garden and ornamental garden were located close to Morval House, across the road from Churchtown. In the eighteenth century a full-time gardener was employed at Morval House, and estate accounts mention cold frames for growing 'cowcumbers' (Pounds 1973). In the late eighteenth to early nineteenth century, the garden of Morval House underwent considerable restructuring, and by 1846 the kitchen garden there had been replaced by ornamental gardens.

The property now known as Churchtown is shown in these early maps as consisting mainly of orchards. Estate records of the eighteenth century show that large quantities of cider were produced on the estate, and it seems likely that these orchards provided the apples. Cultivation of fruit and vegetables continued until the 1960s. The tithe map of 1846 and Ordnance Survey first and second edition maps (of 1888 and 1907 respectively) show the area covered by trees, probably apple orchards. The area labelled *arboretum* had been cleared of trees by the late nineteenth century.

The Walled Garden

Structure

The shape of the walled garden is best described as an inverted U-shape with a wall across the bottom of the 'U'. This comes about because the side-walls are built into, and supported by, the hillsides at the apex of the valley. The curved, north end wall lies across the narrow end of the valley, and is unsupported. This curve, joining the two side-walls and facing south, presumably maximises the potential warming effect of the sun by focusing the heat. The two side-walls are symmetrical. One of the most striking features of the construction is that the base of each of the side walls lies on the same contour, in spite of the acutely sloping nature of the surrounding land. The result is that the top of the main part of the walls is level. By contrast, the wall at the south end of the garden, is straight. It is built across steeply-sloping ground, so that there is a drop of about 2 metres between the sides and the centre; the top of this wall thus has a marked, but symmetrical, downward curve. The walled garden encloses an area of 0.22 ha.

The curved north end wall is built entirely of brick, but has been modified to accommodate a lean-to glass-house. In this region, it is 3.7 metres high but to the east, above a 1.8 metres high door that leads to the work area to the north of the walled garden, the height of the wall is only 3 metres. This part of the wall has slate capping. Another door in the apex of the curved end of the garden leads into an external building that houses the apple store and the gardeners' room. Old photographs show a chimney projecting above this wall, and a stove that heated both the vinery and the other greenhouse is located in this building below the apple store. On the inside of the garden below this curved wall, the soil has been dug out to a depth of about 60cm. This depression is lined with slate, and formed the floor of the original vinery.

The lower courses of the side-walls are built of stone, with the upper parts constructed entirely of brick. The height of the stone part varies along the length of the walls but is never more than about 1m, and tapers off towards the north. In parts of the West Country, fruit walls were originally built of cob with stone footings, but these proved unstable (Gray 1998). It is possible that this was also the original structure of the walled garden, and that earlier cob walls were replaced by brick, retaining the stone footings. An alternative explanation for these stone footings is that they represent remnants of old field walls. Certainly the line of the wall on the east side is continued in the field wall running from the potato store and alongside the 'cherry wood'. It is also indicated as a field wall on the 1846 tithe map.

The bricks used in the construction of the main walls, are handmade, and measure 25.4cm x 6.4cm x 10cm. Around 50,000 to 60,000 are estimated to have been used in the construction of the walled garden. They probably date from before 1840. The origin of these bricks is unknown, but there was a brickworks near Looe that existed until the middle of the nineteenth century. The bricks are laid in Flemish bond. The brick walls, with the exception noted above, have no coping-stones. The walls were thatched in the early part of the twentieth century, but there is no evidence that this was the original form of capping. However, some walled gardens were thatched in order to provide shelter for fruit trees, and this is a possibility here. The south- and west-facing walls contain holes in the brickwork which may have been used for fastening fruit trees or vines.

Several attempts have been made to deal with the instability of the garden walls. Pillars, one brick thicker than the rest of the walls, are spaced at regular intervals along the walls. Both side walls are built into the hillsides, which provide support to the brickwork over much of its length. The result is that the height of the walls outside the garden is less than that inside, which is on average 3.7m. Due to the slope of the hillside towards the south, on the east side, the height of the east wall that projects above soil level varies from about 1m at the north end to the full height of 3.7m at the south end by the potato store. By contrast, the hillside behind the west wall does not slope very much to the south, so that the height of this wall above soil level varies from 2.15m at the north end to 2.25m at the south end. The height of the wall has made it unstable, and there are five buttresses placed at intervals along the outside. Three of these are constructed of stone and are

slate-capped, and may be contemporary with the wall. Two of the buttresses are constructed of concrete and are modern.

The wall along the south side that closes off the garden is completely different to the other walls. It is constructed of stone with a brick capping and, as already mentioned, is built across the greatly sloping centre of the valley, so that the top is markedly curved. There is a drop of about 2m between the bottom of the wall where it meets the side-walls, and the path level in the central gateway. The stonework is not keyed into the brick wall at the east side, but is keyed-in on the west side. The height of this wall inside, at 2.9m, is also lower than the others; outside the earth has been piled up to form flowerbeds, so that the visible height of

Fig. 56 Aerial View of Garden showing the U-shaped walled garden
(© Mrs Angela Kitson)

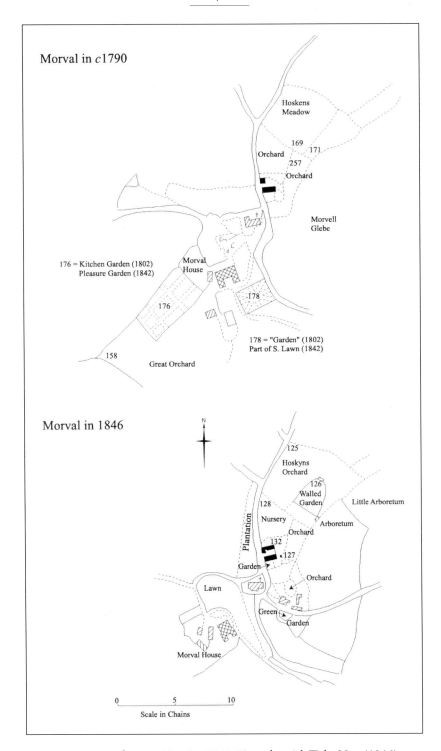

Fig. 57 Morval Estate Map (c.1790); Morval parish Tithe Map (1846)

the wall is about 1.9m. There are also concrete buttresses on either side of the gateway; these have been built since the 1960s.

The main entrance to the walled garden is an arched gateway at the centre of this wall. The opening is 2.2m wide and 2.4m high, and the arch is lined with modern brick. The opening originally contained a planked wooden gate, but now contains a white-painted picket gate. It leads to the central path that runs the length of the walled garden.

History

It is not known precisely when the walled garden was built. Some speculation has surrounded this. Earlier reports have suggested a date of 1753, on the basis that a lead tank inscribed with that date was found in the derelict vinery in the 1960s. However, the origin of this lead tank is unknown, and it could have been placed in the vinery at any time. The hand-made bricks used for the garden walls have been given a pre-1840 date. Detailed accounts were kept at Morval House until about 1800, but no mention was made in these of the purchase of the very large quantities of bricks required for construction of the walled garden.

A garden design dating from the late eighteenth century, showing plans for a walled garden, is amongst the Morval archives. This plan, which shows parallel walls or terraces near a lake, and a gardener's house, clearly does not relate to Churchtown, but may have been intended for the garden of Morval House. Although it does not seem to have been executed, it reveals that the idea of a walled garden was contemplated at that time.

Mention is made in documents of around 1800, and on the estate map, of a kitchen garden close to Morval House. There is no record on the same estate map of the walled garden; instead the area is shown covered with trees and described as orchards. In 1793, the picking of strawberries and raspberries at Morval House is recorded, and in 1794, gooseberries, peas and beans in the kitchen garden there. In 1816 the planting of vines is recorded. In 1820, land use records make no mention of the walled garden, but show the area now occupied by the walled garden as being 'orchard'. About the same time, changes were taking place in the gardens at Morval House, and various plans were drawn up.

Fig. 58 Walled garden showing detail of its shape and construction
(© Mrs Angela Kitson)

In about 1813, a wall was built through the kitchen garden in Morval House. By the time of the Tithe Map of 1846, the kitchen garden had been replaced by a pleasure ground. There is no sign of an alternative kitchen garden near Morval House, but the walled garden is clearly shown on this map. The walled garden appears on all subsequent Ordnance Survey maps from 1888 until the present. The apple store, built onto the curved end of the walled garden, and the potato store, also appear on the Tithe Map. It therefore seems most likely that the walled garden was constructed between 1820 and 1840.

Mention is made of a vinery around 1900, and a derelict vinery was found against the south-facing, curved end wall in the 1960s. However the form of the window glass suggests that the vinery did not date from much earlier than the late nineteenth century. This does not rule out the possibility of an earlier structure on the same site; indeed the boiler, used for heating the vinery, was housed beneath the apple store. An earlier heated structure against this wall is therefore a possibility. Another greenhouse with raised beds, having heating pipes running beneath, was also present at the north end of the walled garden, and heated by the same boiler as the vinery. This greenhouse probably dated from the early part of the twentieth century, and its remains were removed in 1998. Restoration of the walled garden in the 1960s involved not only clearing the land of brambles and removing the derelict vinery, but also constructing buttresses to support the walls and replacing the rotting gate.

The sheltered situation of the area now occupied by the walled garden is ideal for fruit growing, and it is clear from the orchards present in the eighteenth century that full advantage was taken of the site. At the same time, as was customary at this period, the kitchen garden was close to the manor house. In the eighteenth century, fruit was grown against parallel walls arranged in an east-west orientation, similar to the plan drawn up for Morval (Campbell 1996). In the early nineteenth century, the fashion changed to 'landscaped' gardens, and kitchen gardens were moved out of sight. This period coincides with the reorganisation seen in the garden of Morval House. Also at this time, the advantages of brick-walled gardens for fruit cultivation were realised, and many fruit trees were trained up the brick walls to benefit from the warmth stored in the brick. Furthermore, horticultural fashion favoured larger fruit trees necessitating taller walls. In the early nineteenth century, the walls of many kitchen gardens were built to heights of 3.5–4.5 m (Campbell 1996). The height of the brick walls in Churchtown is 3.5 m. There is evidence, from the holes in the walls, that fruit was grown against these walls. Thus construction of the walled garden in the mid nineteenth century would be in accord with developments in other gardens, both nationally and locally.

This study was undertaken on behalf of the Cornwall Gardens Trust and with the permission of the owner of the garden, Mrs Angela Kitson.

References

Pounds, N. J. G. 1973 'Barton Farming in Eighteenth Century Cornwall' *The Journal of the Royal Institution of Cornwall*, New Series VII, Part I, 55

Campbell, S. 1996 *Charleston Kedding – A History of Kitchen Gardening*

Gray, T. 1998 'Walled gardens and the cultivation of orchard fruit in South West England', in Wilson, A. (ed.) *The Country House Kitchen Garden 1600–1950*

Subscribers

Mrs Judith Atkinson
Mr Kim Patrick Auston
Mrs Pauline Baker
Ann Bingle
Emma Birkin
Mrs Shelia M. Brown
Dr R. H. Bruce
Mrs Judie Burman
Mr K. J. Burrow
Mrs D. Butler
Mr James Carter
Peter Child
Mr John Clark
Mrs Mary C. Clarke
Mrs Maureen E. Cole
Tony Collings
Cornwall Archaeological Unit
Mrs Gillian R. Cramer
Mr Graham Davies
Mrs Morny Davison
Lady Violet De Vere
Devon & Exeter Institution Library
Miss June Eckhart
J. C. Edwards
Mr Geoffrey Evans
Mrs M. P. Evans
Exeter City Museums
Mr Peter Fairbank
Mrs June D. Fenwick
Dr Harold Fox
Mrs Wendy Goffe
Mr Derek Gore
Mrs J. Gould
Lady V. Gray
Mrs Clare Greener
Mrs S. Headlam
Veryan Heal
Dr Robert Higham

G. Michael Hitchon
Keith A. Honess
Mr Tom Hudson
Mr Laurence Hunt
Mrs Carolyn Keep
Michael Latham
University of Leicester
Mrs S. Lopes
Mrs P. Mallet-Harris
Mrs Jean Marcus
Mrs Helena Mathew
Mr Brian Le Messurier
Dr Timothy Mowl
National Trust
Dr Alison Newton
Mrs June Parkinson
Mrs R. I. Payton
Mrs Mary Pearce
The Reverend Dr E. Pett
Plymouth City Library
Miss Doris Potter
Mr David Rabson
Mrs Margery Rowe
Mrs Sally Searle
Jo Simpson
Mrs Jenefer Slater
Mrs J. M. Sneyd
Colin J. Squires
Taunton Deane Borough Council
Mrs Stella Turk
Dr B. West
H. Whittam
J. R. Wilks
Mrs Joy Williams
Mrs Julie Wing
Mr Peter Wright
Mrs Letitia Yetman
Professor Joyce Youings